Learn to Read/
Read to Learn

Learn to Read

Read to Learn

POETRY AND PROSE FROM AFRO-ROOTED SOURCES

BEATRICE LANDECK

INTRODUCTION BY CARMAN MOORE

Drawings by Michael Heming

DAVID McKAY COMPANY, INC.
NEW YORK

This book is dedicated to the memory of Ida Baker, who introduced me at an early age to the riches of West Indian culture.

ACKNOWLEDGMENTS

We are grateful to the following for permission to reprint copyrighted material:

On page 7 for excerpt from "Freedom's Plow." Copyright 1942 by Langston Hughes. Reprinted from SELECTED POEMS, by Langston Hughes, by permission of Alfred A. Knopf, Inc.

On page 52 for "Don Gato" and on page 115 for "How Animals Dug a Well." Copyright 1971 by Silver Burdett. Reprinted from MAKING MUSIC YOUR OWN, Book 3, by permission of the publisher.

On page 90 and 91 for "Qué Bonita" and "La Guagua." Reprinted from MUSICA FOLKLORICO DE PUERTO RICO, by Francisco López Cruz. Copyright 1927 by Troutman Press. Used by permission of the publisher.

On page 104 for "Lift Ev'ry Voice and Sing" by James Weldon Johnson and J. Rosamond Johnson. © Copyright Zann Music, Inc. Sole Selling Agent: Edward B. Marks Music Corporation. Used by permission.

On page 67 for "Up on the Mountain." From SONGS TO GROW ON, by Beatrice Landeck. © Copyright Edward B. Marks Corporation.

On page 124 for African proverbs. Reprinted from AFRICAN PROVERBS, compiled by Charlotte and Wolf Leslau. Copyright 1962 by Peter Pauper Press. Used by permission of the publisher.

On page 126 for Mexican proverb. Taken from A TREASURY OF MEXICAN FOLKWAYS, by Frances Toor. © 1947 by Crown Publishers. Used by permission of Crown Publishers, Inc.

On page 135 for "Heaven." Copyright 1947 by Langston Hughes. Reprinted from SELECTED POEMS, by Langston Hughes, by permission of Alfred A. Knopf, Inc.

On page 135 for "Motto." Copyright 1951 by Langston Hughes. Reprinted from THE PANTHER AND THE LASH, by Langston Hughes, by permission of Alfred A. Knopf, Inc.

On page 136 for "My People." Copyright 1926 by Alfred A. Knopf,

Inc. and renewed 1954 by Langston Hughes. Reprinted from SE-LECTED POEMS, by Langston Hughes, by permission of Alfred A. Knopf, Inc.

On page 139 and 160 for "Linstead Market" and "Hosanna" from ECHOES OF AFRICA, by Beatrice Landeck. Copyright 1961 by David McKay Company, Inc.

On page 142 for "Charles Parker, 1925–1955." Reprinted from BE-YOND THE BLUES, by Rosey Pool. Copyright 1962 by Dufour Editions, Inc. Used by permission of the publisher.

On page 101 for "John Henry." Reprinted from JOHN HENRY: TRACKING DOWN A NEGRO LEGEND, by Guy B. Johnson. Reprinted by permission of University of North Carolina Press.

We have been unable to reach the copyright owners of "Jamaica Market" by Agnes Maxwell-Hall and "El Hijo de Conde," "Me Casó Mi Madre," and "Una Vieja Tenía un Niño" as they appeared in RENADIO DEL CANTAR FOLKLORICO DE PUERTO RICO, compiled by Monserrate Deliz. We would welcome any information that would help us to do so.

Special mention of sincere appreciation is made to the colleagues and friends who made possible the completion of this work: Marion Cohan for her loyalty and unflagging support in this venture as well as for her industry in deciphering my illegible handwritten pages and transforming them into presentable copy; Carman Moore for the insight into the current scene he was able to provide, giving generously of time from his ever creative and busy life; Patricia Fosdick for editorial help in focusing the early outlines on purely relevant matters; Evelyn Angel, Ruth Liebers, and Dorothy Uris for reading and rereading the manuscript at various stages and sharing with me their professional expertise; Herbert E. Marks for his wise counsel, his great humanity, and his lovable good humor in putting up with an author-wife. Grateful acknowledgment is also made to the many scholars and educators, too numerous to list, whose research and field work supported my own convictions.

FOREWORD

The pendulum of educational philosophy swings in a great arc from decade to decade. Through the 1940s, its direction was toward the goal of personal development espoused by Progressive Education. This course was abruptly reversed in the late 1950s: after the Russians' launching of *Sputnik*, subject matter with emphasis on math and science was given top priority and the arts fell in low esteem. However, the scientists themselves caused a reversal of this trend, pointing out that children needed more than facts and figures to face the challenges of the space age. Thus the pendulum was set in motion again.

In the 1960s *innovation* was the key word. Reports and surveys proliferated; publication after publication condemned the public school system, proposing reforms and alternatives; and communities pressed for control of local school boards with hopes for better education for their children.

Change is slow in a system of unwieldy size, but it can nevertheless be identified in numerous exemplary classroom practices which are found in schools from coast to coast. In many large cities and their suburbs, changes have taken place. The organization of relatively small community schools and other alternatives to formal education attracted a large number of parents and children. Bilingual instruction was initiated in basic areas of curriculum for Spanish-speaking children. Open and ungraded classrooms (especially at the primary level) gave children an opportunity to learn at their own pace. And special arts-in-education programs multiplied in community centers, successfully demonstrating new approaches for teaching/learning.

The trend of the 1970s is toward moderation of radical innovations with a marked emphasis on basic education. A decade of experimentation has not proved as satisfactory as was anticipated either to faculty or students at higher levels of education. Efforts are now being directed at incorporating positive features of the changes into a more structured curriculum.

Concerned educators weather the pedagogic changes of climate and also change of human attitude, from the melting-pot concept of the 1950s to the recognition of multi-ethnic distinctiveness of the present day. Adopting the positive contributions of each era, they look for ways to balance the values of cognition and character development, of personal creativity and social responsibility. They constantly search for greater insight into how children learn.

Each decade makes its own demands. Throughout the 1960s, black and Latin Americans—through their own efforts—effected a cultural renaissance. They recognized and took pride in the strength of their heritage. But the vast resources of this heritage have not yet been tapped adequately in the mainstream of education.

There is still a need to adjust the curriculum in mainstream education to include cultural resources of ethnic groups whose children attend public schools in large numbers. Parity in the use of curriculum materials is a prime factor in the concept of equality of education. Children of the disadvantaged poor—whose achievement record has been consistently low—have a better chance of success in adapting to the majority culture when their native talents and individual abilities are allowed to develop from the roots of their own heritage.

Nonwhite cultures have characteristics that differ radically from those of middle-class white culture. As a result, many children of these ethnic groups are uninspired by the content of a curriculum designed exclusively for whites, and are unresponsive to methods of teaching based solely on Anglo-Saxon traditions.

The oppressive discipline necessary to maintain order among bored, unhappy children makes adversaries of teachers and students, and school becomes not a place for developing intellectual discipline but a battleground for gaining the upper hand.

To foster a healthy attitude toward learning, materials of curriculum must be made relevant to the needs of those who come to school to learn. It is not enough to provide access to knowledge. A school has the responsibility to help children grasp what they need to know in whatever way is conducive to their learning.

Of primary importance in elementary schooling is that children learn how to communicate in the language of the majority culture. This objective can better be achieved in a classroom in which cultural pluralism is respected. When ethnic materials complement and implement a systematic method of teaching standard English, children of minority cultures gain self-esteem and a degree of stability which helps them become receptive to learning. Over a period of time, they are able to apply themselves in acquiring basic language skills essential to academic growth.

But it takes more than application to learn the rudiments

of any language. Muscles, mind, and heart are involved in the process. The task is lightened when learning time is filled with happy, memorable experiences. Certain salient features of folk cultures afford such memorable experiences. They may be briefly stated as follows:

1. A wealth of folklore accumulated over the centuries expresses real life experiences, furnishing study material that is attractive and of vital interest to children.

2. A customary style of performance encourages community participation in a variety of expressive ways, presenting for classroom use possibilities for collective experiences which allow each child to find his own way to understand subject matter.

3. A traditional call-and-response form encourages individual creativity as well as collective responsiveness. The framework of the form focuses on particular subject matter, initiates creative thinking, and gives shape to individual and group ideas.

Thus the content and structure of the materials and the traditional procedures for developing them furnish vigorous academic substance for a balanced curriculum. Drawing on the diversified materials, past and present, and adopting elements of collective performance allow each child in a heterogeneous grouping to progress in his learning at his own rate, a consequence of inestimable value in working with a class of thirty or more children.

Broadening the school curriculum to include resources of ethnic cultures not only gives black and Latin-American children a fair chance for an education but enriches study for all children. The folklore and contemporary works of Afro-American and Afro-Antillean cultures—now widely available—make a valuable addition to the library. Such books come to life when they are integrated into classroom activities. Academic learning that takes place in formal study is put to use in speaking, listening, reading, and writing and through the expressive arts.

In my own work with children in elementary schools and with students in teacher-training institutes I found that materials from Afro-American and Afro-Antillean sources elicited maximum responsiveness even when classes represented different ethnic groups. I also came to see that the strength of these cultures embraced more than music, which was the area in which I had specialized.

Impressed with the scope of Afro-American culture and the intensity of students' responses, I decided to investigate its wellspring in the West Indies, Central America, parts of South America, and, finally, on the West Coast of Africa. I learned that music is but one attribute of a rich culture mainly concerned with the expression of ideas. Other arts act as a vehicle for an idea, clarifying and amplifying it through individual and group improvisations.

Because of a popular acceptance of music and dance as the sole generating forces of African culture, the value and potency of the oral tradition have been overshadowed. The truth is that poetic speech reaches heights as a folk art comparable to more widely recognized achievements in music, dance, and sculpture. The oral tradition which plays a dominant role in the work of contemporary poets and authors, constitutes a plentiful source of lyric poetry and prose that can awaken a child's senses, widen his horizons, and make education meaningful.

This book is the result of research and study of ethnic cultures as well as of my own experience in teaching and living. It also draws upon the experiences of teachers in the field and the suggestions for curricular reform expounded in myriad books of the 1960s. It attempts to apply the philosophy advanced by leading educators, social scientists, and psychologists to mass education with specific implementation of practical materials and practical classroom procedures that stem from black and Latin-American cultures. Its aim is to broaden the approach to teaching speech, writing, and reading in elementary schools by providing, in the words of a distinguished educator, "richness, variety, and depth to the curriculum."

When the democratic ideal of cultural pluralism becomes a reality in the classroom, all children can take pleasure in learning; they can apply themselves seriously to the study of relevant materials, and can face with confidence the challenge of acquiring an education.

Beatrice Landeck
Westhampton Beach, New York

INTRODUCTION
Carman Moore

The teacher is—with the exception, perhaps, of the politician—
the most controversial professional figure we have. Over and
above every citizen's traditional love/hate feelings for that
mystic parent figure called the Teacher, our cultures have for
the last twenty years felt compelled to voice disappointment
with her/him. At first anxious only about space-related science
studies, critics of the teaching profession soon got around to
every subject, finally settling on reading as the key to the whole
learning problem. And so the money began to flow, the educators' workshops popped up, and the principals' stern words to

their faculties became the order of the day: "Get Johnny's and Alice's noses back into a book. And, oh yes, if you've got the energy, try for Sanford and Willa Mae and Juan and Maria, too."

Fact was that it couldn't be done just like that. Fact was that kids were becoming both dulled and nervous in boring class after boring class . . . that they were saying so . . . that less formal (and perhaps more humanistic) relationships between parents and child were rendering teacher-child relationships less pat, orderly, and predictable . . . and that almost from the cradle television and rock'n'roll music had become the children's major purveyors of culture and their most attractive teachers. Johnny, Alice, Sanford, Willa Mae, Juan, and Maria— same new world for all and same old-fashioned schools. One difference was that the latter four—black and Hispanic—were coming to school with cultural memories and values alien to the teacher and to the text books. The typical white teacher would either ignore the difference and doggedly teach white-middle-American saying, "It's hopeless, but it's a living," or flee to "nice schools" or cry a lot and wait for a new cure, reasoning that polio had fallen and man is in space so why not a perfect basal reader.

As a few teachers have discovered by now, some clues to teaching the children reside with the black and Hispanic children themselves—clues that are largely valid for white students too. Those clues have to do with the African roots of both Afro-American and Afro-Hispanic cultures and the resultant accent on interdependent participation. Those clues also involve mixed-media means of communication by entire communities. Communication—with God, with other villages, with one's own general community, with close friends—is a highly developed complex of techniques and styles in African and post-African cultures. The burden of this art-as-communication is to invent forms that need the thoughts and contributions of everybody. Slavery survived through it. Through it Afro-Latin religions survived and passed on so-called Latin music.

And from it have come most of New World call-and-response vocal forms; the news-reporting musical forms called blues, calypso, and plena; the great twentieth-century vocal form (hiding behind instruments) called jazz; and that audience-participational, media-mixed, protest-cum-philosophy improvisational form par excellence that is rock'n'roll music. Words—a torrent of words, issued forth for millennia—based in firm, ingenious, but simply logical forms are so quintessential to African-rooted cultures! Countless games and song types exist simply to teach and glorify verbal expression. And yet, because those traditions are centered on spoken rather than written words, one hears teachers complain of nonverbal black kids and Latin kids who refuse to learn to read. Nonsense. These are as unreal as the new stereotype of the unfeeling, prideless inner-city teacher. I am convinced that the modern teacher is one of the most mission-oriented and potentially caring professionals in public life. But without help and fresh suggestions he/she will remain also one of the most frustrated.

Beatrice Landeck's approach to reading (and writing) is the result of a lifetime of teaching in the big city and of research in African-rooted music for children. Her suggestions here are as fascinating as they are practical. To her, verbalization rises with music out of the world of sound. She proposes a prereading class activity (which becomes a reading class and much more) called the Word Lab where all manner of word-related skills from the world of childhood can be acquired, sharpened, and enjoyed. This means everything from rhyming games and talking blues and plenas through writing down poems and essays in street language and free-associative imagery. Everything that can be gleaned from the rich art of music relevant to verbal expression, cadence, and sentence sense is called into play in Word Lab. And Miss Landeck's presentation of materials involves precise detailed examples which she has used successfully in her own classes. Most of them are folk tales, folk games, and folk music from African-rooted traditions, whose value in the inner cities should be great.

Learn to Read/Read to Learn, then, is the kind of written material that many a teacher has been begging for. It teems with things the teacher can do on her way to teaching Johnny-through-Maria to read and express themselves verbally. So intriguing are some of the activities that I would venture that the least it will aid the teacher in effecting is an enjoyable class for all concerned. As laid out in this book, it seems altogether reasonable also for the teacher to expect a class that can read and write with enthusiasm. It is created as a manual for the average American middle-class teacher of inner-city children. But I can think of few teachers anywhere who could not gain a lot of twentieth-century-related techniques and confidence by trying on some of *Learn to Read/Read to Learn*.

CONTENTS

All God's Chillun Got Sense

When groups of children play on the streets together, they reveal more of themselves than ever they would in a classroom. Examining the street play of black and Hispanic children, then, should bring into focus certain characteristics of their sensory and cognitive makeup that might be considered a basis for developing work habits in school.

Group play reveals more than individual characteristics. It is a telescopic view of generations of living, shaped by characteristics and mannerisms of parents, by the life style of family and neighborhood, and by identification with cultural background. In carefree games, children unconsciously fuse patterns of the remote past and realities of the present into a union, imitating their elders in style and form of speech and action. The street play of black and Hispanic children delineates a thumbnail sketch of their total environment. For this reason, an account of some real-life examples can aid teachers in finding ways to bridge the chasm between home and school. Realistically observing recurrent patterns of behavior holds clues to effectively planning a program for groups of children that would be both compatible with their life styles and at once conducive to learning.

The *materials* that consistently capture and hold the children's attention suggest subject matter that might serve in the classroom as centers of interest from which topics for study evolve. The *techniques* children employ in learning the routines of their games suggest classroom procedures that would take into account an accustomed way of learning, and which, with a teacher's guidance, would help children acquire the skills they need for reading and writing.

The mind and senses of children are actively functioning in their play. The examples that follow demonstrate that *All God's Chillun Got Sense*. These examples are not to be considered specific suggestions for classroom use; those will come later. But a few anecdotes will throw light on some traditional patterns of play.

Original Versifying

Children find lyric verses a pliable form in playing their games. They often start with a verse they know and through playful manipulation of words devise something of their own. An example of this kind of play was brought to my attention one day in a second-grade classroom of a Harlem school.

The children seemed restless and distracted. To focus their attention I introduced some couplets of a reassuring song in which they could supply a rhyming word at the end of the second line.

> Hush little baby, don't say a word,
> Papa's goin' to buy you a mocking . . . bird.

> If that mocking bird don't sing,
> Papa's goin' to buy you a di'mond . . . ring.

> If that di'mond ring turn brass,
> Papa's goin' to buy you a looking . . . glass.

The children not only supplied the rhyming word as I had expected but they chanted the whole couplet and accompanied their words with a rhythmic clapping game played in pairs. At the end of the third couplet my words began to clash with their words so I gave over to them and listened. Instead of presuming that the ring might turn brass, they chanted:

> If that di'mond ring don't shine,
> Papa gonna buy a bottle of wine.

Traditional Couplets	Children's Version
If that looking glass get broke, Papa goin' to buy a Billy goat.	If that bottle of wine get broke, Papa gonna buy a Billy goat.
If that Billy goat don't pull, Papa goin' to buy a cart and bull.	If that Billy goat run away, Papa gonna beat my boom-dee-ay.
If that cart and bull fall down, You'll be the sweetest little baby in town.	If my boom-dee-ay get sore, Papa gonna take me to the store.
	If that store man say I'll die, Papa gonna punch him in the eye.
	If that store man eye get blue, Papa gonna punch the other one too.

The words these children chanted—variants of the traditional couplets—were undoubtedly made up in play on the streets. I feel sure that when these verses came into being, they were unpremeditated; substitute words and rhymes slipped into place as each child took his turn bouncing a ball or jumping rope. I can visualize the scene:

A group of girls jumping rope; it is Nora's turn. She accidentally chants, if that di'mond ring *don't shine*, and then from her unconscious, rhymes *don't shine* with *bottle of wine*.

Ruby, next in turn, keeps the substitution of *bottle of wine* and quickly senses that *get broke* will work as well with the *bottle of wine* as for the original *looking glass*. She then goes on with the traditional line: *Papa gonna buy a Billy goat*.

Without losing a beat, Rita steps into the circling rope. Stimulated by Nora's mistake and Ruby's recovery, she is ready to add a shocker: If that Billy goat run away (instead of don't pull) Papa gonna beat my boom-dee-ay.

Ella picks up the challenge without hesitation. There is no time to search for words; the rope continues turning and she is next in line. She knows how to end the first line: If my boom-dee-ay *get sore* and the obvious rhyme with *sore* is *store*.

From then on the rhyming is as much fun as the rope skipping, each child trying to outdo the other. The game is repeated with the new verses that are more fun in play than traditional ones. After a few repetitions, all the children on the block are substituting the new lyric for the old.

Versifying for the pure joy of sound and rhythm is a natural and appropriate way for children to express themselves. In this lighthearted rhyme children revealed some of their concerns but without a conscious effort toward introspection which might well have impeded their free flow of language. The stimulus for the flow of words was, in this instance, supplied by rhythmic lines of a familiar verse. The beat was strongly marked, probably by a jump rope hitting the pavement or by the sound of a bouncing ball, but foot stamping and off-beat hand-clapping would have done just as well. Extraneous sounds such as mouth noises and a sharp click or metallic ring—from whatever is at hand—often embellish the basic rhythm.

Call-and-Response Form

When children use the call-and-response form in their play, the procedure for versifying is slightly different from the rope-skipping game mentioned above. A leader starts a familiar verse substituting one or more words for those in the original. Others in the group repeat and/or add to the leader's *call* in response. If two children call an opening line of verse at the same time, the one the group follows wins out; the other aspiring leader tries again at the beginning of the next verse. So the play continues with interaction between leader and group in the traditional call-and-response form.

Children in a black ghetto in Baltimore made up a game using the call-and-response form of "Joshua Fit the Battle of Jericho." They held to the rhythmic structure of the spiritual but changed words and melody to suit their own purposes. The game begins with a girl in the center of a circle as a solo dancer; a leader, supported by others in the circle, clapping hands and stamping, tells her what she is to dance—a pop dance like *juba*, *shimmy*, *jump-up*, *samba*, *frug*, or others they know. The action starts with an introductory verse.

LEADER: *I know a little lady from Baltimore,*
GROUP: *Baltimore, Baltimore.*
I know a little lady from Baltimore
Let's see what she can do!

No matter what dance is improvised, the child in the center is put down (and out) by a teasing refrain:

> LEADER: *Oh, she can't dance, Oh, I know she can't,*
> GROUP: *No she can't, no she can't*
> *Oh, she can't dance, Oh, I know she can't,*
> *Let's see what she can do!*

Solo parts are changed for each verse at which time boys are as eligible as girls as the dancer in the center. The game continues with each leader naming another dance to challenge the soloist.

> LEADER: *Oh, he can't do the limbo, Oh, I know he can't,*
> GROUP: *No he can't, no he can't,*
> *Oh, he can't do the limbo, Oh I know he can't,*
> *Let's see what he can do!*

After the names of usual dances are used up, children make up crazy words to call on the ingenuity of the performer:

> LEADER: *He can't do the* ICKABOGA, *no he can't,*
> GROUP: *No he can't, no he can't,*
> *He can't do the* ICKABOGA, *no he can't,*
> *Let's see what he can do!*

When children play they do not search far afield for subjects. They latch on to what they hear around them and change it enough to make it work for them. The verses the Baltimore children made up bore little resemblance to "Joshua Fit the Battle of Jericho." However, they were not impairing the beauty of the spiritual in thus adapting it but were unconsciously demonstrating their closeness to their heritage by improvising in the traditional way.

Improvisation

The tradition of improvisation is very much alive in black communities today. The harmonic structure of the same spiritual ("Joshua Fit the Battle") was the inspiration for a popular song with a lyric based on a widely told fable of a befriended snake who turns on his benefactor. It was orchestrated in rock style and called "The Snake."

The versatility of spirituals in particular was forcefully impressed on my mind when, within the period of a week, I heard another spiritual sung in three very different settings.

In the morning at school, we improvised words on the spiritual "Hold On," and that evening I heard Pete Seeger sing it in a nightclub. After the first few verses that set the pattern, members of the audience supplied couplets as solos for additional verses with all joining in on the refrain, just as we had done in school. On Saturday of that week, it was performed by a rock group at a civil rights demonstration in Washington, D.C., where its two-line verse gave form to original ideas expressing the convictions and hopes of masses of people.

At a later date, I learned that Langston Hughes had based a poem on that spiritual, called "Freedom's Plow." It is in several sections; this is the last:

A long time ago,
An enslaved people heading toward freedom
Made up a song:

Keep Your Hand On The Plow! Hold On!

That plow plowed a new furrow
Across the field of history.
Into that furrow the freedom seed was dropped.
From that seed a tree grew, is growing, will ever grow.
That tree is for everybody,
For all America, for all the world.

May its branches spread and its shelter grow
Until all races and all peoples know its shade.

KEEP YOUR HAND ON THE PLOW!
HOLD ON! [1]

When black men or women go to the moon, they may well
improvise on "Hold On" to lift them from the earth and sus-
tain their spirit in outer space.

1. Noah, Noah, let me come in,
   Doors all fastened and the windows pinned.

   REFRAIN: Keep your hand on-a that plow,
             Hold on, hold on, hold on.

             Hold on — —
             Hold on — —

             Keep your hand on-a that plow,
             Hold on, hold on, hold on.

2. Noah said "You done lost your track,
   Can't plow straight and keep-a looking back.

   REFRAIN:

3. Keep on plowing and don't you tire
   Ev'ry row goes higher and higher.

   REFRAIN:

4. If you wanna get to heaven, I'll tell you how,
   Keep your hand on-a that plow.

   REFRAIN:

1. Langston Hughes, "Freedom's Plow," from *Selected Poems of
Langston Hughes* (New York: Alfred A. Knopf, 1950).

Such adaptations of a timeless spiritual are but one indication of the vitality of cultural resources that remain vigorous in continuous reshaping.

Ethnic Styles of Performance

Should you stand at the edge of a South Side playground in Chicago and listen to the children at their games, you would hear their palms clapping, their voices lifted in a singsong chant, and see their hips and arms and bodies swaying in rhythms unlike those of any other American children. It is not one song, but a dozen, with patterns of words unheard elsewhere, about corn bread, and stepping out to the dance, and Saturday nights, and all the delights that are not wholly denied them.

Of this great mass of dark-skinned children it has been said that they are culturally deprived, yet here is a culture as spontaneous as it is unrecognized. It tells us again that the spirit of man can still endure under whatever misery and deprivation, on crowded streets and in back alleys where the garbage cans overflow, that here there is even laughter and dance and song.[2]

Black children have a talent for extracting the very essence of their cultural style of performance and for fashioning it for their own entertainment. In referring to earlier days in the rural South, Harold Courlander has this to say in his book *Negro Folk Music U.S.A.*:

The same games were played by Negro and white children in the South even where they were separated by segregation. But although the games and songs were com-

2. Charlemae Rollins, "Foreword" to *I Am the Darker Brother—An Anthology of Modern Poems by Black Americans,* ed. Arnold Adoff (New York: Collier Books, 1970).

mon property, there were sometimes considerable differences in treatment. Negro children brought to them musical concepts derived from the mainstream of Negro musical tradition. They endowed the songs with a distinctive imagery, and often gave the postures and motions of the accompanying action some of the characteristics of Negro folk dancing. Responsive singing, to the accompaniment of rhythmic (often syncopated) hand-clapping, sometimes approximated the effects of adult songs. In other words, Negro children played and sang in Negro style.[3]

One of the chants that appears in Courlander's book gives a vivid impression of this style even in print. Although considered a *game*, it is without prescribed order, action, or melody. It is *word*play, an antiphonic play of words among voices that come from various sources in the room or play area. The whole thing is held together by the rhythm of the words and by a rhythmic accompaniment the children supply.

To begin, each player has a number; when his number is called by the leader he must respond with an appropriate answer without becoming rattled, and then pass the play on to another individual. The chant always proceeds at a good clip, the faster the better, and is accompanied with rhythmic hand-clapping. If anyone misses a beat, he's out, which is an accepted condition of the game that keeps every child alert.

ALL TOGETHER: *1 2 3 and a zing zing zing*
LEADER: *Number one!*
NO. 1: *Who, me?*
LEADER: *Yes, you.*
NO. 1: *Couldn't be.*
LEADER: *Then who?*
NO. 1: *Number five!*

3. Harold Courlander, *Negro Folk Music U.S.A.* (New York: Columbia University Press, 1963).

NO. 5: *Who, me?*
LEADER: *Yes, you.*
NO. 5: *Couldn't be.*
LEADER: *Then who?*
NO. 5: *Number nine!*
NO. 9: *Who, me?*
LEADER: *Yes, you.*
NO. 9: *Couldn't be.*
LEADER: *Then who?*
NO. 9: *Number two!*
NO. 2: *Who, me?*
LEADER: *Yes, you.*
NO. 2: *Couldn't be. Etc.*

I have heard the above chanted with a different rhyming scheme, each child substituting for *couldn't be* a rhyme with the number he holds: number one—*gotta run*, number two—*ain't true*, number three—*not me*, and so on.

This wordplay demonstrates some typical characteristics of the black style of performance: foot-tapping, hand-clapping accompaniment; spontaneous and rhythmic responses within an established pattern; call-and-response form between a leader and, in this case, individuals of a group.

Other ethnic groups are affected similarly by their cultural environment. In city ghettos and rural areas of Puerto Rico as well as in those of Mexico, family life and community life dovetail, with children and adults taking an active part in it together. Even young children are taken to markets, to fiestas, to local celebrations and feasts.

As a component part of such community gatherings music, dance, dramatic ritual, and incessant talking play an important role. The energizing force underlying folk expression is rhythm which is materialized through percussion. Children are enveloped in the sound that permeates the atmosphere and movement accompanies every vibration.

Many of the rhymes and chants of Puerto Rican and Mexican children are variants of those in Spain but, as with black children, each ethnic group carries on a characteristic style of performance to which eyes, ears, and muscles have accustomed them.

Some of the games Hispanic children play have to do with nature or the occupations they remember or have heard about from the homeland; others are the games all children play, enlivened by dancing feet, hand-clapping, finger-snapping and percussive sounds along with nonsense words and syllables that abound in the chants and resound like instruments in the mouths of the young.

Cumulative Form

In the folklore of all Western people, the cumulative form appears in story and song. A cumulative song from Puerto Rico which is a favorite with children is "Una Vieja Tenía un Niño." It is about an old woman who puts in a big bedstead a boy, a dog, a cat, and a mouse. Each one cries in his own manner and the old woman comforts them with the words: "*so, so, so, so, que te quiero yo.*" Following are the first verse about the boy (*un niño*), and the fourth verse about the mouse (*un ratón*), with the cumulation of the other three underlined.

Una Vieja Tenía un Niño

1.   Una vieja tenía un niño,
       una vieja tenía un niño,
       y en la cama lo acostaba;
       el niño lloraba
       y la vieja decía;
       so, so, so, so,
       que te quiero yo.

4. Una vieja tenía un ratón,
   una vieja tenía un ratón
   y en la cama lo acostaba;
   el ratón chillaba,
   el gato maullaba,
   el perro ladabra,
   el niño lloraba,
   y la vieja decía;
   so, so so, so,
   que te quiero yo.[4]

Children love the cumulative form, each verse which repeats the punchline of the verse before keeps them alert until the triumphant recitation of the final lines. This is a trick of concentration that seems to come more easily to the young than to their elders.

Original Cumulative Chant

An example of an elaborate cumulative form appeared in an article in the August 10, 1970, issue of *New York* magazine. The article was titled "The Games New York City Children Play" and was written by Ann Geracimos. As she remarked: "The rhymes seem to come from nowhere, done in unison with dance steps or jump ropes—sounds for sounds' sake."

Each bit she has collected is a testament to children's capacity for humorous verbal expression but in my judgment a cumulative chant beats them all. This is folklore in the making. Ms. Geracimos calls it "an antic opera, played to the hilt, purely for pleasure. All parts of the body can move, shoulders, knees, ankles, eyeballs."

4. "Una Vieja Tenía un Niño," from *Renadio del Cantar Folklórico de Puerto Rico*, compiled by Monserrate Deliz (Rio Piedras: Catedrática Auxiliar de Música, Universidad de Puerto Rico, 1951).

My mother is a baker,
Yummy yum.
My father is a garbage man,
Yummy yum—pee yew.
My sister is a beautician,
Yummy yum—pee yew—la de da de do.
My brother is a cowboy,
Yummy yum—pee yew—la de da de do—
Roll'em up, stick'em up, take'em out.

My auntie is a telephone director,
Yummy yum—pee yew—la de da de do—
Roll'em up, stick'em up, take'em out—hello.

My grandfather is a tickler,
Yummy, yum—pee yew—la de da de do—
Roll'em up, stick'em up, take'em out—hello—tickle,
tickle.

My grandmother is a wicked old witch,
Yummy yum—pee yew—la de da de do—
Roll'em up, stick'em up, take'em out—hello—tickle,
tickle—BOO!

How did such a chant come about? You can re-create the
scene in your mind's eye: children on steps of a stoop about twi-
light, clapping hands, snapping fingers and tapping feet to pass
the time. One child starts to chant *My mother is a baker* and
follows it with the descriptive sound *Yummy yum*. Another
picks up the idea and brings his father into the act, repeats the
yummy yum and adds his own descriptive sound with expression. By this time the form is set; everyone knows what to do
after the next solo—he joins in on the repetitions of the nonsense syllables. And so a cumulative chant is born for all the
children in the neighborhood to enjoy.

It takes a clear mind to accumulate that many words and
sounds in the proper order without losing a beat. But children
seem to have no difficulty remembering what they want to re-

member. Actively and intensively involved in play, they are concentrated and coordinated, functioning as responsible members of a team. There is joy in the joint accomplishment which carries them through to the very end.

Significance of Street Play

For teachers the significance in street play is not in the quality of the end product but in the process of developing it. Children employ a creative process which includes every member of a group. The incentive comes from a traditional procedure of performance reflecting the life style of their environment. Sometimes a folk game or rhythm of a traditional song gives the impetus for making up a game or rhyme with verses brought up to date by substitutions of words or actions that express the day-to-day experiences of the players. Other times, as in the cumulative song, a completely new rhyme is created without the springboard of traditional words or traditional rhythmic frame. But even the new product is created in the same way as the old—through collective improvisation. Children's familiarity with their cultural patterns shapes their actions and enables them without conscious effort to accomplish what they set out to do.

Minority Cultures

The Afro-rooted cultures of black Americans and Latin-Americans have like characteristics. Both are folk cultures evolved and developed from centuries of interactions and exchanges between individuals and groups in small communities. Molded by participatory actions of masses of people, such cultures are markedly different from the culture of white Americans. The greatest difference lies in the custom of collective expressiveness, a characteristic apparent in the life style of adults as well as children.

The call-and-response form, typical of collective expression, has developed a style that is largely poetic, shaped in short rhythmic phrases, repeated with or without variation. A rhythmic phrase—spoken or chanted, beat out by the hands of a drummer or patterned by feet in a dance—arouses a response in kind from the surrounding group. Onlookers spontaneously become participants, playing the part of a chorus as various soloists emerge on impulse from the crowd.

This is the procedure children follow in their play. The pace is kept lively by constant change of leadership. An improvisation by one child motivates another with group accompaniment and response. Children quickly and intuitively respond to a rhythmic stimulus they set up for themselves. Ever alert for what is expected of them, they know how and when to contribute as individuals in a spirit of joyous competition.

Wordplay is their forte. Their language abounds in descriptive *sound* words, unconventional phraseology, and in playful teasing and challenging. They often show great ingenuity in expressing themselves, mimicking the speech patterns they hear—the rhythmic repetitions, the poetic style, the counterpoint of voices.

Resources for the Classroom

These natural endowments, and the riches of the culture from which they spring, are the substance of what can be used in teaching reading and writing to Johnny and Maria. Disregarding the endowments of such children has led nowhere in the past. But building on them seems to me to represent an efficient and efficacious way to bring about the results both black and white parents are trying to achieve.

Materials and classroom experiences that are relevant to a child's life outside the school call for thinking and feeling responses; provoke discussion and experimentation; bring forth suggestions for interesting projects; stimulate students to draw conclusions that relate to what they have been doing, to what they already know, to a broader view of the world they live in. When children work with such materials in a congenial environment, the classroom is full of challenge and triumph. And, what is more, reading and writing become an intrinsic part of classroom life.

We shall see how collective experiences have worked in all grades of the elementary school. But first, we must deal with some popular misconceptions that thwart the normal growth of black and Latin children as well as children of white cultures, whose minds and hearts may be permanently scarred by racial attitudes of the school.

In addition, there are practical details to consider, details of scheduling activities in a curriculum governed by time bells; problems to face that arise from differences in language and from incompatible positions on conformity and creativity that affect classroom behavior.

These are matters as important in helping Johnny and Maria learn to read as are the materials used in teaching. For an enriched environment is one aspect of effective teaching and a democratized classroom is another when learning to read means reading to learn.

The Word Lab | 2

The emphasis on reading, supported by administrators and parents without regard to race or economic status, has resulted in considerable time being allotted in the school day to the reading program. A well-planned program devotes a minimum of one and a half to two hours daily and includes in addition supplementary sessions weekly for special related activities or individualized instruction.

As a scheduled part of the reading program, I propose that the first half hour of the day be spent in Word Lab, a kind of experiential session for *every* grade in which all members of a class would take part. The extra sessions, possibly biweekly, would generally be used for small study groups to work on projects that originated in Word Lab.

A daily experiential session in Word Lab should allow each and every member of a class to participate on his own level of ability. Heterogeneous grouping would be advantageous because diversified materials can be introduced to afford learning experiences that are not based on previous knowledge. Such materials motivate spontaneous responses which supply vocabulary and subject matter for study and give a teacher opportunities to extend children's original contributions into use of the printed and written word.

In a Public School?

The Word Lab can be a part of curriculum in the most conventional school as well as in informal education. Activity programs—especially in the lower grades—are not unusual in the public school. However, the major difference between this approach and other programs is that with the material suggested here, collective experiences are possible in *all grades of the school.* Reading and writing exercises can be devised from sensory impressions to accommodate individual ability and yet be appropriate to the maturity level of students in the upper grades. Statistics on the disparity of reading levels in upper grades of public schools indicate a need for continued work in experiential preparation for reading.

Work in Word Lab supplements an organized method. Thus when an experiential program and an organized method run parallel courses, learning and doing are crossfertilized. A child gains initiative and incentive through production-oriented learning experiences. With a teacher's guidance, the tools needed to accomplish objectives sighted in Word Lab are found in formal studies.

Potential for Learning

There is convincing evidence that inner-city children can be taught to read "provided the priorities are sensible, the effort intense, and the instructional approaches rational in terms of the needs of the learners." This is what Robert R. Wheeler, area superintendent for the Division of Urban Education in Kansas City, is quoted as saying in a pamphlet entitled *Inner-City Children Can Be Taught to Read: Four Successful Schools*. He continues: "We have not accepted the myth that environmental factors develop unalterable learning depression. We believe that so-called negative environmental factors can be overcome with sensitive and responsible teaching." [1]

The pamphlet was written as an Occasional Paper by George Weber, associate director of the Council for Basic Education, an organization "pledged to the encouragement of high academic standards in American Schools." Conclusions were drawn with great caution after a thorough investigation of the reading programs of four successful schools and consideration of those practices the schools were following. In addition to references to specific teaching materials used in each of the programs, to personnel and scheduling, also described as factors in an orderly system were attitudes of teachers and administration: strong leadership, high expectations for children's serious intent and accomplishment, and good atmosphere in the classroom.

Accepting these premises as essential factors in children's learning to read, an orderly system of teaching can be complemented and implemented by experiential opportunities also carried out in an orderly way. A reading program in an inner-city school is enriched by collective experiences that focus on poetry and prose from Afro-rooted sources. Through the many creative responses these materials afford, children become aware of the positive values in their culture; they gain self-esteem and intensify their will to learn.

1. George Weber, *Inner-City Children Can Be Taught to Read: Four Successful Schools* (Washington, D.C.: Council for Basic Education, 1971).

Rewarding results from work in Word Lab require the same degree of belief in children's potential as more formal studies. A deterrent in many city schools is impatience on the part of teachers in trying to move children rapidly from their native manner of expression to school English. Before children move from accustomed usages to a different manner of expression, they need multiple experiences in expressing themselves naturally. Only through speaking do children learn to read, so to be intolerant of neighborhood speech patterns is to discourage an interest in language itself.

If you as a teacher of any grade are looking for informal exercises to help children adopt standard usages, you will find something of value here that supplements a structured reading program: not a step-by-step method but an approach which gives leeway for discovering new pathways for teaching/learning often by following children's leads.

Neither the physical conditions nor needed equipment requires large expenditures of money. Nor are any of the procedures described beyond the capability of a teacher in the elementary grades. The substance of the Word Lab program resides in the poetry and prose that stems from Afro-American and Latin-American sources. Supportive attitudes toward the children who are products of these cultures is the only prerequisite for successful performance.

Cultural Norms

The folk poetry and prose of Afro-rooted cultures has generally not been used to advantage in education. The neglect may be due to the fact that differences in speech patterns between teachers and students loom large on the school horizon. Teachers shy away from literary examples foreign to the majority culture —perhaps assuming they are *inferior*—but in any case not seeing how they can bridge the cultural gap. They nevertheless embrace other cultural practices that do not involve language. Music, for example, accepted as one of the positive values of black culture, is recognized worldwide and integrated into the life style of most Americans. In order to point out how a *difference* between cultural standards does not imply a value judgment on either of them, let me show how a misunderstanding of cultural norms can arise in the classroom even in the area of music.

I have been told time and again by classroom teachers that black children fail to "sing in tune" although they show a high degree of ability in other musical activities. This does not indicate that the young singers cannot carry a tune for when attention is called to the precise tones of a melody, they can sing it as well as any children. But the "out-of-tune" singers are, indeed, indulging in an ethnic preference. Instead of a single tone, they are used to hearing voices sliding and slurring, approaching a tone from above or below the pitch, *bending* the tune a little; instead of roundly blended tones, their ears are accustomed to the sound of individual voices—often of shrill quality—standing out at points of emphasis. Their natural taste leans toward a wider range of tonality, toward a greater variety in pitch and timbre, away from the smooth and sweet.

According to the black's tradition, music is a medium of personal expression amenable to infinite alteration, whereas according to a choral director trained in the Western manner, music is a system of tones to be followed exactly as written.

The world would have suffered a terrible loss had the black man's music been restricted to Western rules of composition before jazz was born. For although jazz employed elements of Western music, it defied the standard practices of the day. Jazz epitomized the Afro-American's love of exotic sound, his concept of its malleability, and the accustomed use of music as an expressive medium of self.

Although the black man's musical tradition is *different* from the white man's, no one would venture to say it is *inferior*. Furthermore, blacks have amply demonstrated that they are capable of adopting Western conventions of music when they choose to do so. Before jazz was accepted by a white public, the

Fisk Jubilee Singers, for example, performed hundreds of concerts in Western style to entertain a white audience for the purpose of raising money for their university. The analogy of music practices to language development is pertinent because verbal expression in black communities is as highly regarded as music by the populace at large. The average citizen appreciates the nuances of language and takes pleasure in *bending* language to be personally expressive. Black Americans are great storytellers as were their ancestors before them. A gift for verbal imagery and abundant humor has created a unique style. The oral tradition of the culture merits respect; children who are products of their environment can be proud of the resources of their culture.

Black English

A pragmatic approach in teaching standard English to black children is to recognize their speech as another language, worthy of the same respect given Spanish. If you have trouble accepting this idea you should read what educator-linguists of the Center for Applied Linguistics have to say on the subject.[2] Their extensive studies have disclosed that black oral expression has its own set of rules; that it employs words from many tongues in a consistent grammatical construction.

A member of the Center, J. L. Dillard, who has taught in universities here and abroad, has assembled a great deal of information in a book called *Black English*.[3] In addition to tracing the history and development of the language and giving examples of its syntax, he maintains that black English "can generate a range of expression just as complex and sophisticated as any other tongue including standard English."

2. Center for Applied Linguistics, 1611 North Kent Street, Arlington, Va. 22209
3. J. L. Dillard, *Black English, Its History and Usage in the United States* (New York: Random House, 1972).

The abundance of lyric poetry in spirituals, blues, and other folk songs, the countless stories, the mythology, proverbs, and parables, the modern plays and poetry that have come from black culture, substantiate Dillard's statement. These are products of an oral tradition of magnitude and substance.

As children gain self-esteem by sensing the respect of their teachers, and as they become familiar with the positive values of their heritage, they will be receptive to other ways of making their thoughts known. But the first hurdle to clear is repression of speech which inhibits development in any language.

To become facile in expressing ideas, children need multiple experiences in speaking and in playing with words and sounds not only in the language that is proper to their culture but in school English too. Such experiences develop an interest in language per se. And, as language perspective widens, a new manner of expression is gradually adopted. It takes time and patience on the part of both teacher and student. Words and usages are not learned in a single instance. They must be spoken and heard time and time again and then used and reused in numerous functional ways before they become part of a child's natural pattern of speech.

Spanish in the Classroom

The Spanish-speaking child also needs to use his own language freely while he is learning English. Otherwise the whole process of his development is cut off until the day he can express himself in the new language. He will learn more rapidly if he supplements structured lessons with aural and visual experiences of an informal nature.

All children learn the sound and meaning of new words through their senses—by manipulating material things, by many repetitions of phonetic sounds and of phrases that come from their native tongue as well as from their work books.

New words are adopted when vocabulary centers around

self—personal names, names for parents, home, school, and natural phenomena; when vocabulary identifies things children can
see—clothing, colors, pictures, and physical objects; and, at an
upper level, when vocabulary describes subjects known through
experience.

At every grade level, children should have the opportunity
to collect in their notebooks words and phrases they have
learned through repeated verbal exchanges in the classroom. The
sentences of experience stories should be written for them if
they are not able themselves and stapled into a personal collection of stories, which they illustrate and title in their own hand.
From time to time children will add to their books a bit of conversation, a short anecdote, telling words of an incident they
want to remember.

When they use words of their own language in class, they
can explain the thought behind the words by drawing a picture,
by acting out the idea, by pointing to an object in the room, by
looking up the words in a Spanish-English dictionary. Discovering new words is a challenge when speaking is encouraged in a
classroom.

It is natural for all children to play with words. In school,
play with words includes words from a child's own vocabulary
as well as from standard lists. Play with words also includes
experimenting with vocal sounds simply for the fun of it. Children are practicing phonetics when they imitate environmental
sounds, play with rhymes, use the voice as an instrument as in
scat, mix up syllables of Spanish and English words, make up
nonsense syllables. Such nontechnical exercises free the spirit as
well as the tongue.

Extensions of Speech

Learning to speak well involves other experiences—musical,
kinetic, and pictorial as well as reading and writing. All modes
of expression interact and help each other, as they do in the

folk arts of black and Latin cultures. The primary focus should be on the spoken word in whatever language the child speaks. Other media serve to make vivid and extend the verbal idea. As a child gains the confidence to open his mouth, his mind begins to open also, freed from boredom and the distraction of conflicting thoughts. He becomes able to look beyond the spot under his feet, to take interest in what he sees and hears. Attractive materials that relate to what children know induce them to learning. Engaging activities stimulate, exercise, and satisfy several faculties at once. Eye, ear, muscles, and mind function interrelatedly, supporting effective recall.

Through it all, one can expect an interchange of languages to take place. On easy terms with themselves and teachers, children have a chance to develop the ability to speak and to listen; to read and to write; to express themselves and enjoy communicating with others.

Words in Full Bloom

Word Lab is the informal part of learning to read. It is the students' time to reveal themselves so that the teacher can help them build on what they intuitively know. It is the teacher's time to find out what motivates boys and girls, to introduce prose and poetry that not only arouse interest but stimulate responses.

The period is given over completely to language and interchange of languages through every means of communication that children can use collectively. Communications are focused on subject matter appropriate to the sophisticated level of the students. The teacher introduces material to get the action going and allows students to keep it going—passing it from one to the other as in their games. They are encouraged to express themselves naturally in whatever way they are able.

Collective experiences call for spontaneous speech, creative writing, movement, work in art and music, as well as listening to stories, poems, favorite recordings, and students' reports and essays. Children are doing and listening in an atmosphere brightened by laughter, singing, music, thoughtful discussion, and withal memorable learning.

In such an atmosphere, interesting projects are initiated on subjects that children choose to investigate further. Extra weekly sessions give the opportunity to pursue the subject in depth: in research or writing reports on research to bring back to the class; in looking over books on classroom shelves or in the library in order to select a poem or a story for class reading; in working out details of a dramatization or a musical accompaniment for a class poem or project; in writing or rewriting a poem or short composition on a subject that rose out of a class discussion.

Children are thoroughly competent at any age of the grade school to carry out their chosen projects in accord with their abilities. Since in Word Lab they are not required to meet previously established standards, they choose assignments commensurate with their maturity. Through these independent contributions they learn to work with their peers and come to respect the importance of social responsibility.

The result of teamwork is reported or demonstrated to classmates in Word Lab. During these recitals of group accomplishments, teacher and children work together to develop class objectives. In doing so, future collective experiences are mapped out and new projects and goals are envisioned.

Materials and procedures for collective experiences that intensify the will to learn are described in detail in the following chapters. So too are procedures described that involve reading and writing as a natural consequence of engaging experiences.

Classroom Environment

In a lively classroom, suggestions for class study come from people—from all the people in the room, teacher, aides, children—and from often-changed objects and decorations that have been prepared to arouse children's interest.

The physical environment of the room includes things that children of ethnic groups want particularly to explore. Walls are decorated with lines of poetry and prose from the cultural repertory. Familiar words then catch the children's attention and whet their curiosity to discover more in the context. Books, magazines, and printed matter about records they like lie around on open shelves for the same purpose.

The usual equipment of the classroom is augmented by articles related to the background of black and Latin children: special art materials, ethnic dress-up clothes, typical instruments of their heritage. This kind of equipment is for classrooms of all grades, not only for those of younger children.

A listing follows for setting up your Word Lab with extra material appropriate to this approach:

> Children's Personal Possessions
> > Individual notebooks
> > Card file for recording collected vocabulary
>
> Open Shelves in Classroom
> > Plentiful supply of relevant books for browsing, reading, and borrowing
> > Pamphlets and ethnic magazines for upper grades
>
> Walls of Classroom
> > Teacher-made charts on which are written titles or first lines of verses from children's repertory
> > An extensive list of challenging assignments for individual choices
> > Posters and photographs of modes of transportation, types of primitive housing, children of other lands, animals of folktales, etc.
> > Book jackets, items of school events, newspaper clippings, etc.
> > Samples of children's art work and writing
>
> Additional Art Materials
> > Whittling materials

Materials for making masks and props for plays
Ethnic dress-up clothes
Additional Materials in Music Lab
Small record collection of soul music, gospel, jazz, and
concert music by black and Latin composers
Selection of following instruments: pairs of sticks,
hand drums or bongo, floor drum, cymbals, triangles,
pairs of maracas, tambourine, ordinary things that
make scratching sounds and ringing sounds, steel
drum (commercially made), chromatic xylophone,
kalimba (thumb piano), tin whistle, harmonica; and,
in upper grades: guitar, ukelele, and 4- or 5-string
banjo

Discipline

Discipline is a subject uppermost on the minds of public
school teachers. The general feeling is that instructing children
would be a simple matter if a teacher did not have to contend
with disciplinary problems. But objective observers of the public
school system have indicated clearly that quality of instruction
and classroom behavior stem from the same root; that unruliness
is more often than not a child's way to call attention to himself.
Children who feel left out register their protests either by going
into a shell or by climbing the walls, neither recourse conducive
to learning.

Generally speaking, children of minority cultures need help
to orient to a school foreign to their life style. One way of helping them adjust is to introduce quality materials from ethnic
resources for study, relevant materials that build a bridge between what children of ethnic groups know outside the schools'
walls and what they can learn within.

The majority of black and Latin-American children are accustomed to behaving properly in their homes. They are also

accustomed to order in the rituals of community living in which they customarily take part. The order implicit in their cultures calls for playful variations within its prescribed shape. This sense of order can exert itself in the classroom when given a chance to operate.

We know how responsive and inventive children can be on their own when involved in their play. Arguments and dissension between individuals are resolved by their peers in order to preserve the tempo of their games. Involvement in the familiar patterns of their play allows for no disruptive influences.

Concentration on the task at hand can be expected behavior if the situation in which it normally occurs can be duplicated in the classroom at least to a degree. When enthusiasm is generated by relevant materials and reinforced by worthwhile activities, children are responsive and productive; they do not need rigid controls to keep them in order. The materials and the activity together impose the discipline.

Activity for its own sake—aimless or trifling—has no place in the classroom. The same can be said about the overused word *creativity*. Productive experiences rarely result from setting children loose and suggesting that they be "creative." Without the impetus of stimulating materials children are apt to flounder and not know what to do. For creativity springs from fertile ground —not from a vacuum. Its impellent power may come from various sources; in this case, from cultural patterns which are joyfully acted out over and over again. However, in large classes were there no framework to focus their efforts, creativity might well be dissipated and end in chaotic behavior.

One aspect of work/play in Word Lab entails recognition of structural form. *Form* in activities is reassuring especially when it supplies a framework for personal and original expressiveness. It is this characteristic in the Afro-American resources that makes them so useful in the public school classroom. They are invested with orderliness in which there is ample opportunity for freedom of expression.

Freedom of expression is never an end in itself, however,

nor does it lead miraculously to the attainment of skills. Evidence is mounting that "Free Schools," in which there are no boundary lines to define expressiveness, have not achieved the success they anticipated in raising the academic level of children of minority cultures.

The position taken by an author-teacher in a popular book of the 1960s—that a teacher *waits* for children to reveal what they want to do—seems to me thoroughly impractical in a public school situation. Since the purpose of children's presence in school is to learn, teachers need not only to awaken interests children may not even be aware of but, further, to direct their responsiveness in the productive channel of gaining academic skills.

Another deterrent to achieving expected behavior from children is superficiality on the part of a teacher. Many a sound educational principle has failed in practice when a teacher cut off an activity or a discussion before the essence of the problem had been dealt with. A treatment of subject matter that does not probe beneath the surface to challenge thinking and feeling responses from children shows a distrust of their innate sensibilities and life experience. Why should they try to prove themselves if nothing is expected of them?

On the other hand, too much repetition during a single session—even if to explore various phases of learning—drains vitality from a piece of material and may lose children's interest. It is often wise to head toward one objective on a plateau of learning with various digressions that support the conclusion to be reached. Review of particular subject matter can profitably occur many times during the term with different values highlighted each time a familiar piece is introduced. In that way, children have the pleasure of relating to something familiar without finding it tedious. In fact, review is a splendid learning device for it reinforces children's learning of basic skills and affords slow learners another chance to grasp what they missed the first time around.

But however interesting and stimulating schoolwork may

be, one cannot ignore the fact that in some classes a teacher finds a child too personally disturbed to take part in class activities. If the problem is severe, the child needs more help than a classroom teacher can give unaided. But a teacher will support a therapist's approach by patiently helping the child build self-esteem, by relieving pressures and fears, and by offering a chance of success in cooperating with classmates.

Such an approach benefits all individuals in a class. Those with lesser problems are gradually drawn into collective activities when they see the satisfaction their classmates are experiencing. Maintaining order in a classroom then becomes a matter of involving children in what they are studying and being confident that they will meet rational expectations in accomplishing what they set out to do.

Speech Improvisations in Verse Forms

Ha-Ha, This-a-Way

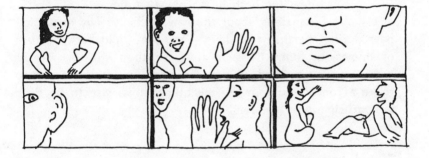

Lyric verses may be spoken or sung but it is an old and honored custom to recite poetry either with or without musical background. The rhythm and the number and length of lines of a musical form traditionally give a performer a frame for improvisation, which is the function lyric verses serve here. Of course, when music is added, it heightens the dramatic and expressive quality of the delivery, a feature of importance elsewhere. But for children in elementary grades, the poetry itself may be the focal point.

In the classroom, children voice the words in whatever way

is natural to them, often with a variety of vocal sounds. En-grossed in a euphonious combination of words, they speak, chant, or sing a familiar or impromptu tune, and may interject wordless sounds as a mark of their enthusiasm. Such spon-taneity is encouraged because it indicates children's involvement with the rhythmic structure of the words.

Telling them what to say or how to say it checks their spontaneity and furthermore inhibits development. When inter-est in verbalizing is at its height, a teacher finds opportunities to turn attention to standard usage of English without direct teaching.

Beginning a term in Word Lab with improvisation on verses, reading aloud, and playing recordings or tapes of popu-lar music gets things off to a good start. These are the stimuli that promote immediate participation of students and acquaint them with a new approach to teaching/learning.

Don't be anxious about those who choose not to partici-pate during the first few days. They may hold back because of shyness or contrariness. In any case, they will be aware of what is going on and at some moment will feel impelled to make a contribution. In the meantime, it is wise to let their nonparticipation go unremarked.

Vocal Improvisations

A verse from the Bahamas, "The Wind Blow East," is a great one for a collective experience in Word Lab because it invites participation of all children (despite language differences) through vocal *sounds* rather than words. It encourages children to take part in a natural, unrestrained way, albeit within the prescribed frame of call-and-response.

Sights of a windy day—clothes blowing on a line, trash swirling in the street—singled out by a child might occasion its use. In introducing the verse, don't spoil the fun by revealing more at the beginning than the alternation of voices. "When

I tell you the wind is blowing, you tell me how it sounds" is all the preliminary needed. Once all children are interpreting the wind howling as each individual hears it, introduce the verse.

VERSE (in conversational rhythm)

LEADER: *The wind blow east . . .*
GROUP (freely imitating the sound of wind):
Whoooooooooooooo-oo
LEADER: *The wind blow west . . .*
GROUP (as above): *Whooooooooooo . . .*
LEADER: *The wind blow* THE SUNSHINE *right
down in town.*
TOGETHER (with a marked steady beat; notice that there
are no words to line out; the group repeats the leader's
words, a wave of the hand will give the cue for join-
ing in):
Oh, the wind blow THE SUNSHINE *right
down in town;
Oh, the wind blow* THE SUNSHINE *right
down in town.*

Word Substitutions

THE SUNSHINE is actually the name of a ship that was blown *right down in town* by a hurricane.[1] It is a suggestive key word for substitutions, calling to mind other weather changes the wind causes and physical things that are blown about. Children have heard the sound of the wind; they have seen the results of its blowing. In response to a question, they readily supply words for a variety of things that have been blown "right down in town." For example:

---

1. Beatrice Landeck and Elizabeth Crook, *Wake Up and Sing* (New York: Marks-Morrow, 1969).

Oh, the wind blow my red shirt right down in town (or right off the line).
Oh, the wind blow my pa's shirt like a balloon.
Oh, the wind blow my sissy's skirt—cover her face.

The words children supply become their personal vocabulary for practice in reading and writing. Children keep a record of their own words and others that appeal to them on filing cards which they refer to in other periods.

Another verse form I have used with good results is from the West Indies. I began by asking the children if they had ever heard Harry Belafonte sing. They had indeed. They mentioned "Matilda," "All Day, All Night, Mary Ann," "Stop the Carnival," and a song about a remarkable little donkey called "Tingalayo." The antics of Tingalayo suggest word changes to children.

REFRAIN: *Tingalay-O!*
                Come, little donkey, come;

                Tingalay-O!
                Come, little donkey, come.

VERSE 1:   *My donkey walk, my donkey talk,*
                My donkey eat with a knife and fork.

REFRAIN: *Repeat*

VERSE 2:   *My donkey eat, my donkey sleep,*
                My donkey kick with his two hind feet.

REFRAIN: *Repeat*

Catching on to the scheme of the verses they knew, a few questions about rhyming words brought forth the following:

3. My donkey sing, my donkey hum,
   My donkey play on his little round drum.

4. My donkey laugh, my donkey cry,
   My donkey wink with his little right eye.

5. My donkey bray, my donkey say,
   My donkey he like to eat some hay.

Spanish-speaking children in the class knew "Tingalayo," too, for it is popular throughout the Caribbean. It has few words to learn so other children in the class wanted a try at the Spanish words.

REFRAIN:

Tingalay-O!
Ven, mi burrito, ven!

Tingalay-O!
Ven, mi burrito, ven!

VERSE:

Burrito si, burrito no
Burrito come con tenedor

Sound and Sight

The Spanish words of the refrain were written on the board, next to those of the English so that the eye could support the ear. Class interest was keen enough to match the two, an idea that originated with two children who were doing just that.

The children saw that in both languages, the refrain started with the same word, *Tingalayo*. Then they quickly discovered that *ven* was the word for *come* and *burrito* the word for *little donkey*.

Later when the verse was written on the board they recognized that the Spanish verse was not like the English verse for it started "Little donkey (*burrito*), yes, Little donkey, no." But they were stopped there because the word *come* in the verse of the Spanish version looked like the word *come* in the English refrain. Those who knew Spanish laughed and explained that the two words did not *sound* alike; that the line meant "Little donkey eats (*come*) with a fork (*con tenedor*)."

Reading Game

Interest in the two versions lasted many days; the children repeated them often in Word Lab. The idea for playing a game with the English version was suggested and called "Pin an Action on the Donkey." The first line of the verse, *My donkey walk, my donkey talk*, had been written on a chart which was now fastened to an easel.

Also, children had written the words they substituted for the original on their filing cards to keep for their permanent collection. When they played the game as they often did in the supplementary periods, each child would choose one of his cards to tack on the chart covering the original word. For example, *eat* would cover *walk*, *sleep* would cover *talk*, and so forth.

Because the game was child-initiated and worked out by those interested without my interference, enthusiasm and gaiety accompanied learning. Later, the "Donkey" game was often played with other verses that called for a single word substitution, but it was not renamed.

"Mary Was a Red Bird" is a song familiar to most teachers in the lower grades. Like the others it presents verses that give a pattern for word substitutions. Substituting name, color, and clothing for those in the original verses often leads to discussions that waken senses of touch, smell, and taste—not to mention some good common sense.

Mary was a red bird, red bird, red bird,
Mary was a red bird, all day long.

"Why do you suppose Mary was a red bird?" Because she wore a red dress, a red hat, red shoes, red gloves and even made a red cake, each descriptive detail and its repetitions furnishing another stanza.

When asked "Where'd you git yo' dress fum?" (also shoes, or gloves and even *ingreemunts o'* de cake) the answer given is:

Got 'em fum de dry goods, dry goods, dry goods,
Got 'em fum de dry goods, all day long.

"Dry goods" are scarcely the words children would use today, but *bodega, chain store,* or *groc'ry* fit the rhythm equally well.

Words for a Sentence

Children personalize the verse by substituting their own names and articles of clothing and those of classmates. The short sentences "Henry wore a blue shirt" and "Amantha wore a green skirt" supply words for reading. Colors and articles of clothing are listed on the board in separate columns. "Can you match them with the name of someone wearing that combination?"

Writing is a part of the activity too. Every young child takes pleasure in writing his own name as the subject of a short sentence. If he has models on the board to work from, he can soon learn to write that he *wore a red* (or yellow) *shirt* or *dug a deep hole* or *kicked up dry leaves*. The structure of the original verse gives form to the children's own ideas.

Boys and girls are attracted to such verses partially because of the element of absurdity in them. Children become involved in learning when they match the written symbols on the board with what they have said in their substitutions and then use the words in writing short sentences. This simple folk lyric opens several possibilities in future repetitions for sensory learning beyond recognizing colors.

The subject of clothing brings up the "feel" of different fabrics and contrasting hard materials involving a whole new vocabulary of descriptive adjectives. Here is another opportunity for interchange of languages. Encourage Spanish-speaking children to give their word of description, writing it on the board if they are able. Compare the English and Spanish, making the experience of double value to all children in the class.

The idea of Mary being a *bird* might easily start a discussion about the different physical attributes of people and birds and why being a bird means being happy. How far this topic is taken depends on the maturity of the children but it does offer possibilities for short essays of a paragraph or two by those who have learned to write. Written during the supplementary periods, these essays read aloud in Word Lab would stimulate other children to try their hand at such an endeavor.

And the word *cake* stimulates conversation on various subjects including what children don't like to taste and smell as well as what they do like. Words, words, words in full blossom result.

Trains

Children are readily involved in learning when an activity follows from and is related to a subject they have brought up themselves. The subject of trains, for example, arises in every classroom of the lower grades. It may be initiated by discussion, by a picture or drawing, by a train sound made by children in play, by a story or an incident concerning trains related to the class by a child or by a spontaneous dramatization of a train.

A good follow-up when the subject of trains has been introduced is "New River Train," a number rhyming verse. After the rhythm is established by chanting the first verse, children

call out words to rhyme the end of the third line of succeeding
verses (as underlined below).

SOLO: *I'm riding on that New River train,*
CHORUS: *I'm riding on that New River train;*
SOLO: *Same ol' train that brought me here*
CHORUS: *Gonna carry me home again.*

SOLO: *Honey, you can't love one,*
CHORUS: *Honey, you can't love one;*
SOLO: *You can't love one and <u>have any fun.</u>*
CHORUS: *Honey, you can't love one.*

SOLO: *Honey, you can't love two,*
CHORUS: *Honey, you can't love two;*
SOLO: *You can't love two and <u>still be true</u>* (for
        example).
CHORUS: *Honey, you can't love two.*

The rhyming with consecutive numbers may go on to *ten* or
more or it may skip aften *ten*, adding *two, three, five,* or *ten* at
a time in each verse just for the challenge of adding quickly in
rhythm.

Children know many ways to embellish a train rhyme such
as adding sound effects made with voice, hands or feet; acting
out the train, sometimes adding a "car" for each verse; using
percussion instruments, again in a variety of interpretations.

When I feel it is time for a last verse, I end with:

> *Honey, you must love all,*
> *Honey, you must love all;*
> *You must love all both tall and small*
> *Honey, you must love all.*

These verses (up to ten) with illustrations by Lucy Hawkinson, have been made the subject of a book called *That New*

River Train.[2] What a motivation for a beginning reader to recognize in print what he already knows! This is how a child gains the confidence he needs to *read.*

Numbers in Lyrics

A verse all children love presents problems in elementary math:

> *Green Bottles*
>
> There are nine green bottles a-hanging on the wall,
> There are nine green bottles a-hanging on the wall,
> And if one green bottle should accidently fall
> There'd be ———— green bottles a-hanging on the wall.

The substitution of different numbers of bottles that "should accidently fall" necessarily changes the number "a-hanging on the wall." The challenge of quick thinking so as not to lose a beat is what makes the verse attractive. This is a great verse for holding children together during a *waiting* time. If the waiting is going to be long, start at 99 instead of 9.

Some other lyric verses in the black repertory using numbers are "Band of Angels" and "By'm By,"[3] and "The Holy Baby."[4] Children may know these or others. If it seems timely to pursue the reading and writing of numbers in the context of a verse, suggest that children look over a collection of songs or verses to find those with numbers. When they browse through a book to discover something to share with their classmates, their minds are impressed with the idea of turning to books for pleasure.

2. *That New River Train*, pictured by Lucy Hawkinson (Chicago: Albert Whitman & Co., 1970).
3. Beatrice Landeck, *Songs to Grow On* (New York: Marks-Sloane, 1950).
4. Alan Lomax, *The Folk Songs of North America*. Part IV: *The Negro South* (Garden City, N.Y.: Doubleday, 1960).

A fascinating number story to read aloud to children is a fable about counting the number of spots on the Leopard's coat.[5] After many animals try in vain, Rabbit solves the problem by going over Leopard's whole body, saying "light-dark" until every spot has been touched. Then he triumphantly announces that Leopard has only two spots—dark ones and light ones.

Everyone Takes Part

Children of Hispanic background, either from islands of the Caribbean or Mexico, can take an active part in the foregoing type of collective experience. They are supported by visual aids (such as a picture of a leopard in the above fable) and carried along by the rhythm of a lyric verse with its obvious pause for a single word substitution (as in New River Train and others). Through the repetition necessary to accommodate individual contributions, these children catch on to the general pattern and are encouraged to supply their own ideas as they can. Spanish words are written on the board and examined by the class as a whole so that children of all cultures benefit.

But Spanish-speaking children can go beyond this. Encourage them to share with other members of the class verses they know that are similar in construction. The dialogue form is widely used by people of both Spanish and African origin either as a conversation between two people or between a soloist and chorus. It is interesting to note that the soloist is traditionally called *Inspirador*, the meaning and significance of which is obvious.

Many examples suitable for this treatment can be found in other sections of this chapter, notably, for young children, in Playacting and Traditional Games. In addition, in chapter 4 for upper grades under the general heading Improvising in Bilingual Classes will be found *Bombas* and *Plenas* which also supply

5. Edna Mason Kaula, *African Village Folktales* (Cleveland: World Publishing, 1968).

frames for young people's speech improvisations. Others from
La Música Folklórica de Puerto Rico [6] serve the same purpose.

An unusually attractive book for young children to browse
through is *El Toro Pinto and Other Songs in Spanish*, selected
and illustrated (in five colors throughout) by Anne Rockwell.[7]
Once children are caught up in the enthusiasm of speaking,
chanting, singing verses in Word Lab, their appetites for verse
will demand considerable nourishment. Turn to them for suggestions from their ethnic background. Most children know
name games like *Susan, Susan bo Busan*, Sesame Street rhymes,
traditional songs like "He's Got the Whole World in His Hand,"
"Had a Dog His Name Was Blue," "We Shall Overcome," "This
Little Light of Mine," "When the Saints Go Marching In,"
"Coming Round the Mountain," and a host of others, possibly
including a long ballad.

Start a class collection, frequently changing charts on the
wall; look through song collections to find lyric verses that can
be treated in a way similar to the examples above. Choose those
that have the following characteristics:

> Repeated short lines (for quick learning of words)
>
> Lively rhythmic structure (for children's finger-snapping,
>   hand-clapping, and foot-stamping accompaniment)
>
> Call-and-response form (for substitutions of original
>   ideas by individuals with participation of class)

Playacting

A story read in Word Lab may inspire a child later to paint
a picture, to mold a figure in clay, or to take part in a dramatization involving most of the class. But a story is also read to be

6. Franciso López Cruz, *La Música Folklórica de Puerto Rico* (Sharon,
Conn.: Troutman Press, 1967).

7. *El Toro Pinto and Other Songs in Spanish*, selected and illustrated
by Anne Rockwell (New York: Macmillan, 1971).

enjoyed for itself, for the aesthetic pleasure that the sound of language gives a listener.

Listening to a teacher's diction as a story unfolds impresses the sound of standard English on children's ears. Alert to every detail, they absorb the sound of language and recognize the meaning of words in the context of the story—words that well may be beyond a controlled vocabulary. When reading a story in verse form, there is no need to interrupt it to explain a word; the rhythm of the piece and the repetition of words and lines hold a child's interest to the end when a word or idea not understood can be clarified.

Ballads

A ballad is a story in verse form. Many ballads hold endless fascination for children. Although I have heard student teachers complain of their length, I have yet to hear the child who vouchsafed leaving out a single stanza.

Because of the story line, children rarely think of changing the words. But they do participate in the telling of a story in other spontaneous ways:

They join in on a repeated phrase and on the refrain.

They supply a key word at the end of a line, usually a rhyming word.

They interject words or sounds to express their involvement during the story.

They contribute a stanza they know by "reading" it from a chart or printed page.

They act out one of the stanzas alone or with a classmate (role playing is a vivid form of communication understandable to children who speak different languages).

Two verses of the perennial favorite "Mister Frog Went

A-Courtin' " will demonstrate the possibilities of participatory listening and single rhyming word responses:

> TEACHER: *Mister Frog went a-courtin' and he did ride,*
> CLASS: *Um-hm! Um-hm!*
> CLASS: *Mister Frog went a-courtin' and he did ride,*
> TEACHER: *Sword and pistol by his* — side
> CLASS: *Um-hm! Um-hm!*
> TEACHER: *He rode up to Miss Mousie's door,*
> CLASS: *Um-hm! Um-hm!*
> CLASS: *He rode up to Miss Mousie's door,*
> TEACHER: *He gave three raps and a very loud* — roar
> CLASS: *Um-hm! Um-hm!*

As the plot thickens and the teacher's voice adds a theatrical note, group responsiveness heightens. Lines like *Mister Frog would laugh and shake his fat sides* always elicit vocal and imitative action from listeners. Although thoroughly attentive, children can't sit still when they hear about the little flea (in some versions, Colonel Flea) who danced a jig with the bumblebee or about a fluffy yellow chick who ate so much it made him sick. The scene changes as scary vocal responses accompany the line *The next came in was an old tom cat.* No matter how many times the ballad is repeated, young children always greet it as if they were eager to hear how the story unfolds.

Dramatizing such a ballad with its many verses gives every child in the class a chance to act out one of the stanzas either as the sole character in the verse or with a friend as one of the two. Children are given a written copy of the two lines of the verse they choose as a "script" to work from. Like professionals they won't need it when they perform for others but the script will help them remember the words as they plan and rehearse their parts. A subtle way to get across the idea that reading is supportive rather than confusing!

An illustrated book of the lyrics of "Frog Went A-

Courtin' " [8] is a good one to have on the shelves for children to discover. The lucky one who comes upon it—either by recognizing the pictures or the words—will be quick to share it with classmates, likely boasting that he/she can read it through. Other ballads, equally attractive to the young, can be found in song collections mentioned in this chapter and also in source books listed in the bibliography.

Romances y Romancillos

If Spanish-speaking children in the class know some ballads —*romances* or *romancillos*—it would be a joy for them to share one of the stories with their classmates. A similar repetition of short phrases and words of the refrain (often nonsense syllables) make it possible for English-speaking children to join in after a first hearing. The eye aids the ear if the Spanish words that are to be repeated are written on the board.

The story line of a *romance* can be conveyed to those who don't understand the words either through mime by the Latin children or by their translating the short lines of a stanza into English. When several classmates get together in a supplementary period to work on a single stanza, they can help each other and, if trouble develops, turn to the teacher (or a pocket dictionary) for a single word.

Several *romances* with repetitive lines and nonsense syllables as refrain appear in *Renadio del Cantar Folklórico de Puerto Rico*, collected by a teacher in the public school system, Monserrate Deliz.[9] "El Hijo del Conde" has a refrain line *caramba!* which makes participation by all children irresistible. Although no lines are repeated in this *romance*, the stanzas are short. Each can be acted out by one or more children who speak the lan-

---

8. John Langstaff and Feodor Rojankovsky, *Frog Went A-Courtin'* (New York: Harcourt Brace Jovanovitch, 1955).
9. *Renadio del Cantar Folklórico de Puerto Rico*, compiled by Monserrate Deliz (San Juan, Puerto Rico: Universidad de Puerto Rico, 1951).

guage as a scene in the story and thus portray the meaning of
the Spanish words.

Unlike "Mister Frog," this story does not describe a wed-
ding but ends with a mother's anger because her practical daugh-
ter refuses to marry the son of a count who has no money.

El Hijo del Conde

El hijo del Conde, ¡caramba!
me escribió un papel,
que si yo quería, ¡caramba!
casarme con él.

Yo le contesté, ¡caramba!
en otro papel,
que hombre sin dinero, ¡caramba!
no trata mujer.

Tanto estuvo el hombre, ¡caramba!
con aquél papel,
hasta que mi madre, ¡caramba!
lo llegó a saber.

Me cogió mi madre, ¡caramba!
me llevó al corral,
con la disciplina, ¡caramba!
me quiso acabar.

A la cocinera, ¡caramba!
tal coraje dió,
que ollas y platillos, ¡caramba!
todos los rompió.

Subject Matter

Another *romance* that Señora Deliz points out as the favorite of all her groups is "Me Casó Mi Madre." In this, stanzas
are made up of only two lines, each repeated, and with a typical
refrain of ¡*Ay, ay, ay!*

The fact that this particular story is most often chosen by Puerto Rican children would seem to indicate a wish to identify with the realities of the grown-up world even if in a lighthearted manner. The ballad is not about courtship but about married life. In translation, it goes like this: "My mother married me, a young and pretty girl, to a boy I did not love." The boy proves faithless, slipping out at night to visit *la otra mujer*. When he returns, he calls out in much the same loving way as at the other house: "Open the door, my dear one, open the door."

Perhaps we underestimate the breadth of children's interests, too often restricting classroom materials to those *we* think they *should be* interested in. But children have big eyes and big ears—especially those who live in close quarters. There is no reason to censor or dilute the substance of their interests.

The first two verses of "Me Casó Mi Madre" should suffice to remind children of this Puerto Rican ballad if they know it. These two verses also make clear the pattern of repeated lines and the refrain which is what the class would join in on. There are, however, fourteen verses in the original.

Me casó mi madre,
me casó mi madre,
chiquita y bonita,
¡ay, ay, ay!
chiquita y bonita.

Con un muchachito,
con un muchachito
que yo no quería,
¡ay, ay, ay!
que yo no quería.

In working with children anywhere, it is wise to go directly to source books or to an authentic collection for ethnic materials. Field collectors put down what they hear without removing the "guts" from the original. A teacher uses his own discretion in choosing materials from such sources keeping in mind that no child of elementary school age wants to be babied today.

Reading and Writing Challenges

If children don't respond to the suggestion of sharing *romances* they know with the class, surprise them one day in Word Lab by having written on the board the title, or a couple of key words, either from a refrain or first line of a verse in Spanish that you have copied from a book. Help the children decode the words and then ask them to try to recall the verse. If this doesn't jog their memory, it might at least whet their appetite to know more of the story. Let a group of Spanish-speaking children use a supplementary period to discover the story from the book and then work out a way to convey its meaning to other members of the class in Word Lab.

This game strategy can be applied to discovering ballads in English. Or techniques of reading and writing can be reinforced by using a familiar ballad in a challenging game. In the latter case, write on the board the key words of two ballads for begining readers; of three or four ballads for children who are more able. When children discover what the words stand for, they can choose the one they want to act out.

Such a project might be initiated as follows:

These words name (or are the refrain of) two ballads you know. When you discover what the words represent, you can vote for the one you want to act out.

Don't tell your neighbor when you recognize this one (pointing to one set of words)—keep it a secret. When you raise your hand, I'll know you are ready.

When enough hands are raised, call on one child to give the answer. Ask another child what he thinks and so on until the class agrees on what the words represent. Call on as many different children as time allows until the class as a whole can identify the ballads.

Then take a vote on which ballad will be acted out. Groups

of children will work together on one stanza or on two if two are needed to complete a "scene." Suggest that the leader of a group with the help of members of his group use extra time to write out a "script" for the stanza they are working on. The next day they can choose the characters to be played, and improvise the actions. When the scenes are put together by one group after another, the class acts as chorus on the refrain, which should, of course, be written on the board.

Thus activities that center on children's interests put to use the skills they are learning. Efforts are redoubled to make sense out of symbols when they aid a child in what he is doing instead of frustrating him.

Cultural Identification

Some Latin ballads have been translated into English. One that seems to delight children is the Mexican ballad "Don Gato." I don't know whether its fascination lies in details of Don Gato's predicament or in the miracle of his return to life after death, but a fact worth mentioning is that resurrection is a recurrent theme in Latin mythology.

"Don Gato" differs from the other ballads discussed in that it has longer lines and no repetitions except for the refrain *meow, meow, meow*, so it does not lend itself favorably to children's reading or writing. However, such ballads serve another important function. The familiar ring of a few Spanish words in a rhythmic verse invites Spanish-speaking children's participation. They want to follow the jist of the story—which is also typically Latin in humor—and need to focus attention on the English words as they are read by the teacher.

This ballad bears a good deal of repetition. Spanish-speaking children should be encouraged to act out the stanzas with the other children helping to make clear any word they do not understand. Thus language study becomes a joint project for both groups in the context of a happy experience.

Don Gato

1. Oh, Señor Don Gato was a cat,
   On a high red roof Don Gato sat.
   He went there to read a letter,
   meow, meow, meow,
   Where the reading light was better
   meow, meow, meow,
   'Twas a love note for Don Gato!

2. "I adore you!" wrote the lady cat,
   Who was fluffy, white, and nice and fat.
   There was not a sweeter kitty,
   meow, meow, meow,
   In the country or the city,
   meow, meow, meow,
   And she said she'd wed Don Gato!

3. Oh, Don Gato jumped so happily
   He fell off the roof and broke his knee,
   Broke his ribs and all his whiskers,
   meow, meow, meow,
   And his little solar plexus,
   meow, meow, meow,
   "¡Ay caramba!" cried Don Gato!

4. Then the doctors all came on the run
   Just to see if something could be done,
   And they held a consultation,
   meow, meow, meow,
   About how to save their patient,
   meow, meow, meow,
   How to save Señor Don Gato!

5. But in spite of everything they tried
   Poor Señor Don Gato up and died,
   Oh, it wasn't very merry,
   meow, meow, meow,
   Going to the cemetery,
   meow, meow, meow,
   For the ending of Don Gato!

6. When the funeral passed the market square
Such a smell of fish was in the air.
Though his burial was slated,
meow, meow, meow,
He became reanimated,
meow, meow, meow,
He came back to life, Don Gato! [10]

Following Children's Leads

Because children are complex human beings with individual traits and developing personalities, what reaches one child may leave another untouched. For this reason it is essential that the classroom supply a rich environment offering a great diversity of materials and of active learning experiences.

Variety is the spice of classroom life. Don't fall into the trap of planning a sequence of events as a daily routine. Always knowing what to expect causes some children to close their ears and eyes. Instead be prepared with a number of resources that can be mustered as occasions for them arise.

Follow children's leads once they have been introduced to a variety of materials and different ways of learning. One day they may choose to spend the whole period of Word Lab on a single piece and at the end of the scheduled time may want to form groups to continue work on the same thing in supplementary periods. Another day, and in another mood, the class may need a constant change of pace to satisfy their general restlessness; they may not become deeply involved with any one activity.

However, if you can envision good learning strategies in attractive material, don't discard it because it was not immediately seized upon by the children. Introduce it again at another time in a different context and possibly stressing a different facet of the piece or the learning experience. Techniques of teaching

10. *Making Music Your Own,* Book 3 (Morristown, N.J.: Silver Burdett, 1971).

can often be learned from closely watching and responding to children's moods and reactions.

Discussing Spirituals

The lyrics of spirituals must be regarded as pure poetry. They are a product of group wisdom and record metaphorically the thoughts and feelings of black people in this country for a period of two and a half centuries. Because the lyrics portray ideas in imagery of familiar objects and actions, children can identify with them through a literal interpretation of the words. Discussion of the literal meaning leads them to a deeper understanding of the poetry.

Many spirituals use trains as a symbol of freedom from slavery. Get from children what a train means to them. Discuss with them the size of a locomotive, its blackness, the speed at which it travels and its ability to start and stop, its power to pull many cars, what great distances it goes, and what it passes on the way. Let them talk about their own experience with train rides or their uncle's or cousin's. Have some children find pictures of trains in books in the room.

Discussion before a dramatization adds seriousness of purpose to what children portray in movement. As they start thinking, they will sense the urgency of the train, its power of locomotion, and will want to be transformed into this powerful free spirit by becoming the train themselves.

Literal Interpretations

"Git on Board Little Chillun" gives children the opportunity through dramatization to feel the liberation of spirit that trains symbolize. The sound of its language as well as its literal meaning suggests percussion accompaniment. The colloquial expressions and the warm invitation implied in the phrase "There's room for many-a-more" includes everyone in a class.

REFRAIN   *Git on board little chillun,*
       Git on board little chillun,
       Git on board little chillun
       There's room for many-a-more.

VERSE   *The gospel train is comin'*
       I hear it close at han',
       I hear the car wheels movin'
       And rumblin' thru the lan'.

(Repeat REFRAIN)

VERSE   *The fare is cheap and all can go,*
       The rich and poor are there,
       No second class aboard this train,
       No diff'rence in the fare.

(Repeat REFRAIN)

Descriptive movement is truly a universal language. Children who know little or no English can take part in the dramatization and later draw pictures of a train in their notebooks. They genuinely appreciate the help of English-speaking classmates in titling their pictures with English words. Encourage children of different backgrounds to help each other. To extend the experience—and incidently show that written symbols have meaning in any tongue—ask a child to write the Spanish word *tren* on the board next to the English word *train;* discuss how they resemble each other both in appearance and sound.

There are other well-known spirituals on the subject of trains with which children identify through dramatization. It is interesting to note that the concepts expressed in the lyrics of spirituals can be as meaningful today as they were centuries ago when they were created. One of many examples of contemporary significance in spirituals is in "All God's Chillun Got Wings."

"All God's Chillun Got Wings" taken literally usually implies air flight to today's children, again transferring to them a sense of freedom in their identification with a plane, a chance to fly to some "heavenly" place.

> I got a plane, You got a plane
> All God's chillun got planes.
> When I get to heav'n, gonna fly in my plane
> Gonna fly all over God's heaven.

> Heaven, Heaven,
> Ev'ry body talkin' 'bout heaven, ain't goin'
> there,
> Heaven, Heaven,
> Gonna fly all over God's heaven.

Pursue the subject further: "If you had wings, where would you fly?" brings forth torrents of words from the articulate child. "I want to hear where Juan or Brenda wants to fly" gives a chance to more timid children to voice their thoughts.

To spread the discussion over several days, groups of children may work in supplementary periods deciding how they will convey their ideas to the rest of the class; shall they give a word description of the place they would like to go—shall they act out the means of transportation to get there (plane, car, bike, train, etc.) or shall they show in movement or words what they would do when they arrived there? Once the decision is made, they go about planning and then present their interpretation in Word Lab.

The next time this spiritual is brought up in class, children will be better able after a literal interpretation of the lyrics to dig deeper for what *Heaven* implied to those who sang it long ago.

From Literal to Figurative

There are two stories to follow up train and plane dramatizations: one is a fable about Tortoise who wanted to fly [11] with the disastrous consequences that when he tried, he fell to earth and cracked his shell; the other, titled "All God's Chillun Had Wings," is told as a memory of slavery and may be found in *The Book of Negro Folklore*.[12]

The two stories are very different in feeling. The fable tells of Tortoise, who, wanting to fly, hides in a bag of tobacco leaves which Osprey is to deliver as a present to a friend. When he is high in the air he feels stifled and calls to Osprey to let him down. Osprey is frightened and drops the bag. The memory of slavery, on the other hand, tells how slaves working in a field were badly mistreated by the overseer. One by one, they took wing and flew away, never to be seen again. Both stories have deeper meanings than the recital of incidents. Although the slave story is more profound, the choice between them depends on the maturity level of the group; but either story will provoke discussion and initiate reading and writing projects of value.

Don't put words into children's mouths, but if the word *freedom* comes up in discussion, it might start them thinking about the symbolism of "wings to fly all over God's heav'n." When everyone who wants to speak has had his chance, as a challenge to those who are able suggest that children write a few sentences in their notebooks about the discussion. Some children may find other ways to express their feelings—in painting a picture, sculpting in clay, or making up a percussion composition. The fact that writing is but one way to express ideas should not be underestimated.

11. "The Tortoise and the Osprey," from Geraldine Elliot, *Where the Leopard Passes, A Book of African Folk Tales* (Philadelphia: Dufour Editions, 1963).
12. Hughes and Bontemps, *The Book of Negro Folklore* (New York: Dodd, Mead, 1958).

Variety of Interpretations

But a teacher cannot call the shots in advance. Unless there has been discussion of wings and of planes in relation to "All God's Chillun Got Wings," young children might instead associate *wings* with material things they can possess, such as something to play with. Children in my classes have substituted "a kite to fly," "a drum to beat," "a horn to blow," "a skirt to swish," "fancy shoes to walk," and so on.

A child speaks or chants his substitution in the first short phrase, then the class joins in, repeating the idea and riding it to its conclusion. Some children have wanted to pantomime the idea for the class to guess. In either case both the individual and the class are involved.

Practice in the basic skills of reading and writing attends the activity as it progresses. Different children write the substituted word or phrase on the board as it is expressed in speech or pantomime. In this way all words are recorded for a repeat of the entire "production." Sometimes, instead of speaking or pantomiming, each child's substitution is written on the board for the class to discover and use in context. This is a good suggestion to make on a day after children have had time to think up a new idea that might stump the class. If they are presented with a challenge to look forward to they will work hard to find an unusual substitution and to learn how to spell it. Skills develop slowly but surely in a classroom where *the immediate goal* of reading or writing is an enjoyable activity.

In discussing ways to travel the word *wheel* is bound to be mentioned. A spiritual that uses this word in a different context is "Little Wheel A-Turning in My Heart." Young children think of all sorts of things happening "in my heart": "clock-a-ticking," "drum a-beating," "doll a-crying," to mention only a few sound-words that are often interpreted with percussion. Other phrases that have to do with how they feel (the rhyme with *wheel* probably suggests it) are often interpreted in dance, sometimes with a percussion accompaniment.

Oh, I feel so very . . .

> *lonely in my heart:* (some children think of a cymbal
> lightly touched as a "lonely" sound)
> *happy:* (almost always tambourine)
> *pretty:* (often suggests the clean shiny sound of the tri-
> angle)
> *scary:* (sharp click of sticks or low drum played menac-
> ingly)

Perception is quickened and interest heightened when any
of the dance or percussion interpretations are presented without
words. It takes creative thinking on a child's part to communicate a particular phrase or verse without words; members of a
class are equally challenged to interpret what is being said in
movement or sound. Solo performance and group responsiveness
are thus refined in a shared experience when the subject matter
is child-centered.

Any actions that spontaneously occur as children are so en-
gaged are to the good—stamping on the beat, clapping on offbeats, snapping fingers, making percussive sounds with mouth,
body, instruments or objects at hand; moving in place or around
the room in dance or dramatization. Suggestions for variations
on the basic theme abound.

Spontaneity can be encouraged without fear that freedom
of expression will be abused. For this potent material not only
stimulates creative responses but also contains them within the
limits of the verse form. Responsive actions have a definite beginning and ending, dictated by the materials.

Freedom in supplying words and phrases is subject to the
same kind of discipline. Original contributions are focused on
a particular topic and fall within a prescribed phrase rhythm.
The challenge this presents will add to the fun you and your
class will have rather than detract from it.

Experiences that involve the whole class are conducted during Word Lab where the interaction of children and the tempo of their activities keeps everyone alert. This period is the source of inspiration that motivates the individual and team work that is carried out in supplementary periods. What is produced in the extra periods is fed back into the collective experiences which all members of the class share together.

Traditional Games

Games have a place in the Word Lab, too, for no time for learning is lost in play. On the contrary, games are especially useful for learning language aurally, for children pick up the words without effort. Since one of the best ways to teach any language is in a rhythmic framework, a rhythmic game which involves children actively is doubly beneficial.

An extraordinary collection of "Games, Plays, Songs, and Stories from the Afro-American Heritage" called *Step It Down*,[13] has recently been made by Bessie Jones and Bess Lomax Hawes. The two collaborators conducted a workshop in California for a group of teachers who wanted the valuable material made available in published form.

Mrs. Hawes writes in Note to Parents and Teachers:

Somehow the simple setting down of words and tunes and actions had lost its validity for me; perhaps I have absorbed too much of Mrs. Jones' point of view. The "how" had become more important than the "what" and the "why" most vital of all. So I have tried to write an instruction book which will give some clues to the understanding of all three, in the hope that parents and teachers who may use this

---

13. Bessie Jones and Bess Lomax Hawes, *Step It Down—Games, Plays, Songs, and Stories from the Afro-American Heritage* (New York: Harper & Row, 1972).

book may come to have an appreciation for the totality of this tradition, and not just rifle it for its substance.

The recollections of Bessie Jones' life experiences over a period of seventy years in a small farming community of Dawson, Georgia, as interpreted for teachers by Bess Lomax Hawes, make a book of inestimable value for work with black children.

A familiar song *Shoo Fly*, also a game, has two fine lines in addition to the title line, "For I belong to somebody" and "I feel like a morning star." The only direction given to start the game is to ask children to hold hands and form a circle facing in. From then on it's follow the leader. As in much of the material, the refrain comes first:

> *Shoo Fly don't bother me* (move toward center of the circle)
> *Shoo Fly don't bother me* (move back to original circle)
> *Shoo Fly don't bother me* (move toward the center again)
> *For I belong to somebody* (move back to original circle)

Before the verse (caution children not to drop hands), the leader (only) drops the hand of the child on his left and he and the child on the right raise arms to form an arch. Led by the child whose hand has been freed, the circle of children pass under the arch and form a new circle joining hands again with the leader after he turns under his own raised arm. This action sounds complicated in words but is easily performed. The verse line is repeated often enough to continue through the action.

> VERSE: *I feel, I feel, I feel,*
> *I feel like a morning star*
> (repeated ad lib)
> *So . . .*
> REFRAIN: Repeated in words and action

If the head of the line turns left going under the arch, children will be facing toward the center as the new circle is formed. But it is fun for children if after a repeat of the refrain, the head of the line turns right (to repeat the verse) in which case the circle is facing outward. In fact, it is so much fun for them to move into the circle backwards (twice through one short phrase) that I feel delivered from possible chaos when the pattern of the dance changes the direction outward. Thank heavens for the discipline inherent in structure!

Patterns of Movement

Ring games like *Hokey-Pokey, Little Sally Walker, Loop de Loo, Sissy in the Bond,* and *Bluebird, Bluebird;* line games like *Paw Paw Patch, Amasee, Cock-a-Doodle Doodle Doo;* reels; and hand-clapping games like *Pat-a-Cake* and *The Mocking Bird* call for a sequential pattern of prescribed action in which a child loses thought of himself in the routine of play. Other games however require individual originality such as the statue game *Up on The Mountain,* (p. 67) and *Ha-Ha, This-a-Way* (p. 63). But these categories and names of familiar games merely scratch the surface. Hundreds of others supply fresh and exciting material for classroom use.

American Games for Latin Children

There are many games that English- and Spanish-speaking children can enjoy together, the Spanish-speaking children quickly catching on to the sense of the words through the action. *Ha-Ha, This-a-Way* is one of these. It initiates word changes described by play acting. It may be played in formation with the soloist in the center of a circle or, and I think preferably, informally with children sitting wherever they are in a room. A child rises to make his contribution.

The refrain is gay with an actual laugh in it:

Ha-ha, this-a-way
Ha-ha, that-a-way
Ha-ha, this-a-way
Then, oh, then.

The verse strikes a different note, calling for a phrase describing an action. The child who contributes a verse acts it out so that everyone understands what he is saying:

SOLO: *When I was a little boy, little boy, little boy,*
When I was a little boy eight * years old,

* Substitute the age of children in class.

SOLO: *Papa taught me fisting, fisting, fisting,*
Papa taught me fisting to save my soul.

REFRAIN: *Ha-ha, this-a-way*
Ha-ha, this-a-way
Ha-ha, this-a-way
Then, oh, then.

SOLO: *When I was a little boy, little boy, little boy,*
When I was a little boy eight years old,
Mama taught me pounding, pounding, pounding,
Mama taught me pounding to save my soul.

REPEAT REFRAIN

SOLO: *When I was a little boy, little boy, little boy,*
When I was a little boy eight years old,
Mama didn' whiff me, whiff me, whiff me,
Mama didn' whiff me to save my soul.

REPEAT REFRAIN

Children will have innumerable ideas to describe what papa,

mama, teacher, and preacher have taught them at a given age "to save their soul."

Puerto Rican Games

On the other hand, Spanish games can give Latin children the chance to assume leadership by introducing a game they know. No explanation is needed. In playing the game, non-Spanish-speaking children follow the action as they do on the streets and get the sense of the words from the activity.

Ha-Ha, This-a-Way may bring to mind a well-known Puerto Rican game, *San Serenín*. Instead of "Ha-Ha, this-a-way" it says "*Hacen así—así, así, así*" which means practically the same thing. It, too, is an acting-out game, traditionally of household chores. Also, as in *Ha-Ha, This-a-Way*, it may be played informally or with a child in a circle or leading a line. Single word substitutions describe the action.

San Serenín

REFRAIN: *San Serenín*
              a la buena, buena vida,
VERSE: *Hacen así, así las lavanderas* (laundresses)
              así, así, así.

REFRAIN: *San Serenín*
              a la buena, buena vida,
VERSE: *Hacen así, así las planchadoras* (pressers)
              así, así, así.

Another widely known Spanish game is *Ambo Ató,* the first line of which has been corrupted to *Ambos a Dos* (both together) in Puerto Rico and *Amato* in Mexico. The nonsense syllables of the second and fourth lines of the introductory verse are repeated in each succeeding verse. The second verse asks a child to choose a trade which he does by action as well as words; it is accepted and imitated by the other players. As with all this material there are many variants not only in lyrics but in ways of playing the game. Adults learn along with the children, a situation helpful to those in the class who need building up.

1. *Ambos a dos,*
(REFRAIN)   *matarile, rile, rile*
     Ambos a dos,
(REFRAIN)   *matarile, rile, ron.*

2. *Qué oficio le pondréis?*
(REFRAIN)   *matarile, rile, rile*
     Qué oficio le pondréis
(REFRAIN)   *matarile, rile, ron.*

3. *Le pondremos zapatero, (shoemaker)*
     matarile, rile, rile, etc.
          (Repeat 1st line then 2nd refrain line as above)

4. *Ese oficio si le gusta,*
     matarile, rile, rile, etc.

5. *Celebremos todas juntas,*
     matarile, rile, rile, etc.

The English game *London Bridge* may suggest a similar one to Spanish-speaking children. *A la Víbora* is played the same way under a bridge of raised hands. The child who is "caught" makes a choice between two objects which determines which side he will be on. A tug of war usually ends the game.

Line Game under a Bridge

A la víbora, a la víbora de la mar,
   por aquí voy a pasar;

Por aquí yo pasaré y una niña dejaré;
de estas niñas cual será la de alante o la de atrás?
las de alante corren mucho, la de atras se quedará.

Pase, misi, pase misa
    por la puerta de Alcala
Pase, misi, pase misa
    por la puerta del canda-o-a-o, a-o

Not only does it build the morale of Spanish-speaking children to take the lead in a class, to be able to introduce games that are likely unfamiliar to their classmates and yet easily followed by them, but it also helps all the other children in the class to know that there are many ways to communicate ideas. Encourage Spanish-speaking children to suggest other games they know, tag games played in circle form (like *Bluebird, Bluebird*) such as *Arroz con Leche* and *Doña Ana* or the Mexican version *Doña Blanca* and a pebble game also played in a circle, *El Florón*. It is good to get selections from the children themselves but if you want to see a large collection of Puerto Rican games in print as well as other songs of various types, get hold of *Renadio del Cantar Folklórico de Puerto Rico* (cited earlier; see note 9) a book that should be in every school library.

Decoding for Fun

A choosing game similar to the one suggested for ballads gives children a little practice in decoding words. Titles or first lines of three familiar games are written on the board. Children are told that the words symbolize three *games* they know. (By naming the category of the written material children are able to focus their thoughts on a particular area of familiar experience thus limiting the possibility of error. In fact, I have often given the name of titles out of order and asked beginning readers to identify the order in which they are written. This is an exercise not a test. Its point is to give each individual child a *purpose* in successfully decoding the written words.)

The class studies the key words of one of the games quietly, trying to match the written symbols with the *sound* of words they hear in their inner ear or silently form with their lips. No one is called upon to read a title aloud until there is a fair showing of raised hands. When the writing reveals to a majority of the class titles of all three games, a vote is taken to determine which shall be played first. *Shoo Fly, Skip to My Lou,* and *Up on the Mountain* (below) are examples of three that beginning readers can recognize.

Up on the mountain, two by two,   (3 times)
    Rise, Sugar, rise!

Let me see you make a motion, two by two,   (3 times)
    Rise, Sugar, rise!

That's a very poor motion, 'deed it is,   (3 times)
    Rise, Sugar, rise!

Let me see you make another one, two by two,   (3 times)
    Rise, Sugar, rise!

That's a very fine motion, 'deed it is,   (3 times)
    Rise, Sugar, rise!

Exploration of Phonetic Sounds

We have seen that bilingual play calls attention to words and their meaning and supplies a useful vocabulary for reading and writing. Creative play can also direct children's attention to speech sounds, to the sound of consonants and vowels they will work with in phonic exercises. A verse that calls for filling part of a line with nonsense syllables, animal sounds, or other sound vocalizations is especially adaptable for this purpose. A teacher can guide the play toward practice of the particular consonants or vowels needed at the time. *Skip to My Lou*, because it is familiar, will serve to demonstrate. However, any other of this type that you know or that the children suggest will also do.

Playing with Sound

We often used the first two verses of *Skip to My Lou* to deal lightly with a child who is out of place in a line. This is the kind of teasing that resolves a situation quickly.

1. TEACHER: *Lost my partner, what shall I do?*
   GROUP: *Lost my partner, what shall I do?*
                   Lost my partner, what shall I do?

   REFRAIN LINE: *Skip to my Lou, my darling.*

2. TEACHER: *I'll find another one, prettier than you.*
   GROUP: *I'll find another one, prettier than you.*
                   I'll find another one, prettier than you.

   REFRAIN LINE: *Skip to my Lou, my darling.*

To lead to wordplay, another of the verses is on a wall chart:

Flies in the buttermilk, shoo, shoo, shoo
Skip to my Lou, my darling.

Children readily suggest substitutions of different creatures for *flies* and locations and sounds appropriate to their subject:

Pigs in the pigpen, oink, oink, oink
Cows in the barnyard, moo, moo, moo
'Gators in the water, slish, slish, slish
Snakes in the schoolroom, hiss, hiss, hiss

The *s* sounds are good practice for children of elementary school age. Once on this tack, a speech lesson follows with material supplied by the children. Visual representation of the sound to be explored is written on the board in each instance.

Sister on the stoop—kiss, kiss, kiss
Slidin' on ice—swish, swish, swish
Snappin' my fingers—snap, snap, snap

Everyone joined in on snapping fingers. So to continue the making of sound effects and to change the *s* sound to *sh*, I contributed "Shovin' my shoe" which brought forth a loud chorus of "shush, shush, shush" from the class.

Thus, one sound combination or word in a phrase suggests another and no one wants to stop the exercise. *Shoe* suggested its companion *sock.*

Socks on the stove—sizz, sizz, sizz

and *sizz* led us to experiment with the buzzing sounds which are particularly attractive to children. "Ever hear bees?" always brings the immediate response "buzz, buzz, buzz." Stressing the *zh* sound gives speech a solid base. At the same time, it is such fun to play with the sound in the mouth that it opens up a whole new avenue of expression often far away from the original verse that started the activity.

Percussion

Practice in sounds can be continued another day with a variation that keeps interest high: producing sounds with drum accompaniment. For words like *zigzag, zero,* and *zipper* (each word written three times in a phrase line on the board), children take turns making up a rhythmic phrase on a drum. They are quite perceptive in catching the character of the meaning of each word in the rhythm they play for it. *Zero* almost always get a single drum beat for both syllables of the word, repeated in a slow rhythm three times; *zipper*, a series of short taps in a fast rhythm; and *zigzag* is invariably interpreted in a sharp movement across the drum in a zigzag pattern. After listening to the phrase the first time it is played, children speak the word as the drummer repeats his pattern. Then a child plays one of the three patterns and others guess what the drum is saying by calling out or by pointing to the word phrase on the board.

Reproducing the word *zing* calls for a pair of cymbals and a loud crash. The preparation for making the crash gives the cue for voicing the word so that the sounds occur simultaneously. The trick is to hold the word as long as the sound hangs in the air.

Vibrations

A child asking why the sound lasts so long brings up the word *vibrate* and here we are on another tack with a whole new class of things to explore. "How many things can you think of that vibrate?" Bells, telephone wires, a tightly stretched rubberband, and a garbage can struck with a stick are some of the first things that occur to children. But this is only the beginning— the beginning of a new awareness that a sensitive teacher can use for months of explorations.

As part of the discussion about vibration, I point out that the *v* of the word itself *vibrates* in the mouth, tickling the lower lip. Children test this new knowledge with words they suggest such as *vegetable, vanilla,* and *van* emphasizing the *v* so that it really does tickle the lower lip. (Any words the children suggest are written on the board for them to look at.)

To examine the *v* sound further, we compare it to the *zh* sound which also vibrates in the mouth. Children discover that the tongue vibrates behind *closed* teeth in the *zh* sound whereas with the *v* sound the teeth lightly touch the lower lip.

Individual experimentation goes on and on, reviewing the

sounds that have been learned to see which one tickles most. This is the moment to introduce the *th* sound of *the* and of *breathe* which tickles the tip of the tongue. Practicing the standard way of pronouncing *the* with an entire class in the frame of an enjoyable activity helps bridge the gap between *de* and mainstream language. We come back to the *th* sound time and again but to avoid undue stress at any one time, we go on to other vibrating sounds: the *j* sound of *jazz, jingle, jive, jockey* engages the whole mouth in the game. Experimentation may be noisy but its beneficent effects are well worth the noise.

Speech exercises of this sort are carried on with a class as a whole. Naturally children experiment by themselves individually in the classroom and out of it but no one is ever singled out to be corrected or "helped." Speech patterns are as intrinsic a part of one's personality as are tonal patterns or pitch in singing. Calling attention to an individual's lack of conformity to standard practice only impedes his progress by making him self-conscious. Everyone in a class needs help to some degree; how far an individual will go on his own or what pattern of speed he adopts depends upon the quality of stimulation he receives in the classroom.

Practice Outside of School

Children are fascinated by speech exercises when they are allowed to experiment with mouth sounds in a childlike way. In order to strengthen recall as well as to promote the habit of practice outside of school, I often ask a question the day following study of a specific sort: "What vibrating sound were you playing with on the way home yesterday?" "Did your brothers and sisters have a good idea for a word with a vibrating sound?" or "What verse (also beginning with *v* as in *vibrate*) kept coming back to you as you were trying to fall asleep last night?" Children like a connecting link between home and the classroom so they take the hint and carry classwork beyond the school walls.

Playing with phonetic sounds aids speech and increases vocabulary. It is of inestimable value to children learning to speak English. Such exercises occur spontaneously as they rise out of a particular piece of material. There is no definite beginning of the exercises and certainly no end to them. Ears are constantly being sharpened and eyes opened when children have time to explore individually and collectively and time to make their own discoveries. What they learn in this way stays with them.

Charles Bell's Work

A brilliant example of how phonetics in a rhythmic framework aids academic learning was reported in the *New York Times*. Charles Bell, a jazz pianist turned teacher, helped boys in a New York public school to learn to read by using phonetic sounds of vowels in a rock'n'roll rhythm. He worked closely with the English teacher and in the following example was demonstrating the vowel *a* as it is sounded in *father*. "There are three sounds for *a*," Mr. Bell said. "*Aah, Aa,* and *Ah,* so we sing"— his fingers snapped and his foot tapped as he launched into a simple melody—"Give me a *ch* with a No. 3 *a*—*ch* (snap) *ch* (snap) *ch* (snap) *cha*."

He added to the *Times* reporter: "Learning doesn't have to be stiff; I want to bring something happy into the black schools. I'm taking the cultural surroundings that these children grow up in and using the emotional forces of this music to grab hold of them."

Devising a Game

Using Mr. Bell's idea, a teacher can devise a game in verse form with rhyming words spelled alike to familiarize children with both vowels and consonants. Children are experienced enough to respond spontaneously to a given line and will accept the challenge of quick thinking in order to preserve the rhythm.

If large letters are given to a child to put on a flannel board, not only will his eye help his ear and lessen the chance for failure but visual learning will go along with the oral game.

A pattern that occurs to me is the following:

LETTERS: *D*   *A*   LATE

Snap fingers at *x*.

        x   *x*   *x*   *x*

LEADER: (snap) *Just take a* D *and an* A *that is long like* LATE

    x   *x*   *x*

Now you make a rhyme and the word is

       x

CLASS: DATE

In the same pattern, substituting the word *short* for *long* as needed, the following consonants and vowels can be studied by sound and sight, with the class supplying the rhyming word on cue.

LETTERS:		
L	*A*	FAST
B	*Ē*	SEE
S	*E*	BET
M	*Ī*	NICE
H	*I*	MIT
N	*Ō*	GO
D	*O*	LOCK
S	*Ū*	DUE
B	*U*	FUN

Providing rhyming words for simple patterns is play to children. If a rhyming word is suggested that doesn't *look like* its mate in spelling, there is an opportunity to point out the variant. When a child writes the words he suggests on the board, the class has a chance to observe those that look alike and those that do not.

Collective Experiences in Depth | 4

In most public schools third grade is the cutoff point for students to learn through their own creative efforts. By narrowing approaches to learning at upper levels, however, boys and girls who have not acquired basic skills of reading and writing are denied many stimulating experiences that would intensify their will to learn.

For these children a creative experience is especially valuable. Simple tasks like recording single words they have suggested for substitutions or writing short sentences that come out of a Word Lab experience are one part of a challenging activity appropriate to their chronological age. In such a situation a child does not feel stupid or backward. A student improves his or her skill while enjoying all the riches of a program. More able students are not held back by the less able in collective experiences. They have the opportunity to probe deeply into a subject that may have been introduced by a child still wrestling with attainment of rudimentary skills. Children interact with each other and help each other when they are involved with meaningful projects. With a teacher's guidance, they work together to reach class objectives that are not beyond realization.

Experiences in Word Lab also feed into a systematic method of teaching standard English. Supplementary periods afford time either for groups of children to work on projects in depth or for individualized instruction when it is needed.

Responding to Work Chants

Chants that have given the impetus for heavy work have tremendous appeal at every age. Youngsters identify with the strong emotions expressed in chants and through their identification give vent to their own feelings with bursts of energy.

Although I try to say as little as possible in a class—for nothing stops the flow of children's words more quickly than teacher's long explanations—I nevertheless sketch a setting for the chants when I find it necessary to do so. For example, some children may not know what function the call-and-response form of chants serves when men are working on a job. A few words describe the scene: a group of workers slowly ready themselves to move a heavy load while their leader chants the solo part. Feeling the rhythm of the chant from the solo performance, the workers take a deep breath near its end and then thrust forward with maximum cooperation as they chant their chorus part. Giving this brief background explains the call-and-response form and sets the stage for reenactment, adapting words and actions to suit a particular task.

"Driving Steel," a simple but strong work chant, has a slow tempo, in what Sandburg calls "hammer swing rhythms." [1] Accented words are underscored.

(Full Voice)
LEADER: *Driving steel,*   *Driving steel,*
CHORUS: *Driving steel,*   *Driving steel.*
LEADER: *Driving steel, man, is hard work I know. (Man, I know.)*
LEADER: *Driving steel,*   *Driving steel,*
CHORUS: *Driving steel,*   *Driving steel.*
LEADER: *Driving steel, man, is hard work I know.*

Other verses follow the same pattern as the first; the chorus repeats the words of the leader as in the first and third lines.

> Treat me right, (*Response*) treat me right (*Response*)
> Treat me right, man, I'm bound to stay all day. (Yea, all day.)

> Treat me wrong, (*Response*) treat me wrong, (*Response*)
> Treat me wrong, man, I'm bound to run away.

> (Almost in a whisper)
> Boss man, (*Response*) boss man, (*Response*)
> See the boss man comin' down the line.
> Boss man, (*Response*) boss man, (*Response*)
> See the boss man comin' down the line.

After a group of children dramatized the original words, a direct question to one child after another, "What heavy work have you ever done?," brought forth a variety of calls and responses including the following:

1. Carl Sandburg, *The American Songbag* (New York: Harcourt, Brace, 1927).

Scrubbin' floors, (*Response*) scrubbin' floors, (*Response*)
Scrubbin' floors, man, is hard work I know . . .
Washin' walls . . .
Luggin' coal . . .
Totin' logs . . .
Diggin' ground . . .
Haulin' water . . .

And so on, the group responding with repeats of the caller's chant.

A rather precocious girl in one of my classes suggested that, instead of children volunteering to take a solo, they call on each other—girl call on boy, boy call on girl—each to show a kind of hard work in any way they chose. That meant that the one called on could act it out, could chant it in rhythm, could draw a picture on the board or write the words. After an outburst of protests from others in the class, her suggestion was modified by changing the performance from solo to group. Several children worked together (mostly boys with boys and girls with girls) to come up with a presentation that combined the media of expression in which they excelled. The class project developed as a contest with the winning team determined by the volume of applause.

Parts of Speech

When original ideas are in full flower, I casually introduce the terms for parts of speech as they relate to children's improvisations. For instance, I might say, "John's action word was *lugging;* the object of his *lugging* was *coal.* Can you think of another object you might lug?" or, "What about another action word to use with *coal?*"

By repeated use, the terms *action word* and *object*, and later *verb* and *noun* (noun as both subject and object), become as meaningful as other words in the vocabulary. When such terms are used to name what children have done, they understand the terms without explanation and are soon using them properly themselves.

In the same way, when children list in their notebooks words or phrases that they or their classmates have used in the context of a verse, the action words go under a heading VERBS, the subject or object under NOUNS. The abler children who volunteer write them on the board. Others copy what they see. In time, more and more children have turns to write verbs and nouns on the board due to sheer perseverance on their part—they want to get into the act.

Research

Work chants often appear in print in various versions, since the collector notates the one he hears on a particular job. The skeletal framework is easily recognizable; the variations are due to one man's extemporaneous changes. Discovering such variations poses a challenging research problem for a child interested in pursuing it.

Children may find work chants in various collections (see Bibliography) to share with the class. "Driving Steel" in the version on page 76 was collected by Carl Sandburg and appears under the title "Hammer Man" in *The American Song Bag* (cited earlier in this chapter). A different chant but known by the same name—probably because work chants are not titled until they are collected—is one of the children's favorites. This "Hammer Man" has for its chorus part only a sound which signifies the workers' expiration of breath as they strike with a blow of their hammers.

Acting out this chant with big movement of the arms falling on *whew* vividly conveys its function. Mark the three heavy steady beats that precede each *Whew* with foot stamping.

Hammer Man

CALL	RESPONSE	CALL	RESPONSE
Take this ham-mer,	*Whew,*	carry it to the cap-tain,	*Whew.*
Take this ham-mer,	*Whew,*	carry it to the cap-tain,	*Whew.*
Take this ham-mer,	*Whew,*	carry it to the cap-tain,	*Whew.*
Tell him I gwine-	*Whew,*	tell him I—gwine.	
I don't want no	*Whew,*	cornbread and molas-ses,	*Whew.* (3x)
Tell him I gwine-	*Whew,*	tell him I—gwine.	
Hurts my pride-	*Whew,*	hurts my—pride.	*Whew.* (3x)
Tell him I gwine-	*Whew,*	tell him I—gwine.	

Discussion

"Hammer Man" and "Driving Steel"—as well as other genuine work chants—launch class discussions because of the sentiment they arouse. Before getting into the historical significance of such chants, it is often wise to start a discussion by relating their themes to children's own lives. Phrases like "treat me right" (or wrong), "bound to run away," "boss man," "hurts my pride" in a *real* chant living men sang on the job touch children's sensibilities.

Discussion of such subjects can lead children to express their own concerns. Do you feel you are treated right? Would you run away if treated wrong? Where would you go? Who is *your* boss man? When is your pride hurt? Any of these questions are on a child's level and are likely in a proper environment to open a floodgate of verbal responses.

After the children have talked about the words of the chants in relation to themselves, they have greater perception of the meaning of the words to the workers who sang them. Listen to them re-create the scene of the steel driver and of the hammer man and explain to you why one feared the boss man, why the other didn't want "cornbread and molasses."

Suggest that children write a few sentences on a subject of their choosing that is related to the chants, either to keep for themselves in the privacy of their diary (notebook) or to share with the class at a future time. Take for granted their need and wish to do this—not as an essay or a paper to be evaluated but as an opportunity to express emotion deeply felt. A teacher shows respect for children not only in believing in their ability but also by recognizing the intensity and breadth of their feelings. When children are taken seriously, they behave seriously.

Speech Exercise

Seriousness in study can be nicely balanced with gaiety considering the great variety that exists in available resources. For example, "Pick-a-Bale o' Cotton," also an energetic work chant, has a bright mood that contrasts with the two chants mentioned above. The first verse sets a rhythm, the second and third as printed here allow for word substitutions, and the last, at top speed, ends the performance with a speech exercise. Well-articulated consonants add to the fun.

SOLO:	1.	*Jump down turn around,*
CHORUS:		*Pick a bale o' cotton;*
SOLO:		*Jump down turn around,*
CHORUS:		*Pick a bale a day.*

CHORUS:	(REFRAIN):	*Oh, Lawdy,*
		Pick a bale o' cotton,
		Oh, Lawdy,
		Pick a bale a day.

SOLO:	2.	*Me and my wife can*
CHORUS:		*Pick a bale o' cotton.*
SOLO:		*Me and my wife can*
CHORUS:		*Pick a bale a day.*

(REFRAIN)

SOLO: 3. *Me and my buddy can*
CHORUS: *Pick a bale o' cotton,*
SOLO: *Me and my buddy can*
CHORUS: *Pick a bale a day.*

(REFRAIN)

In unison as fast as possible, exaggerating the explosive sound of consonants:

> 4. *Pick-a, pick-a, pick-a, pick-a*
> *Pick a bale o' cotton,*
> *Pick-a, pick-a, pick-a, pick-a*
> *Pick a bale a day.*

(REPEAT THIS FOURTH VERSE TO
END CHANT)

Forming the voiceless consonants *p* and *k* (one with the lips, the other in the back of the mouth) in quick succession proves to be a fascinating exercise for children who repeat the *pick-a* ad infinitum with a variety of dynamics. I have seen them quietly working at another task moving their lips almost soundlessly forming the word *pick-a*. Then again I've heard them competing with each other, shouting it in quick succession as loud and fast as they can.

Spanish-speaking children may know an alliterative rhyme they can share with the class. When children invent exercises for themselves, they are more easily made aware of the function of tongue, lips, teeth, and breath in forming sounds, and work at them thoughtfully for the fun of it. Incidentally the exercises improve pronunciation.

If the children's perceptive and cognitive faculties are constantly challenged, a teacher need not worry about the class getting out of hand, even if the children are boisterous. Ear, eye, and muscles are interacting to reinforce each other, and learning is taking place on several levels of consciousness. Sometimes it takes hold through the emotions, sometimes through play or after intensive study, or in a quiet, relaxing activity. As long as there is enough material to elicit a variety of responses, every member of the class will be reached in some way.

Diction Through Percussion

You might want to try another way to call attention to the articulation of consonants by likening vocal sounds to instruments. The quality of vocal sounds in the spiritual "Rock-a My Soul" can be rendered by percussive instruments. Have children consider this by asking them to listen to lines of the refrain spoken with good articulation in a syncopated rhythm:

> *Oh, a Rock-a my soul in the bosom of Abraham*
> *Rock-a my soul in the bosom of Abraham*
> *Rock-a my soul in the bosom of Abraham*
> *Oh, Rock-a my soul.*

"What instruments that you can play would give the effect of these lines?" Suggest that a few children choose instruments from the box of those available and form a rock group. Let several groups "audition" with their instruments while the class speaks the lines.

The solo lines of the verse are different in character. In contrast to the jazzy quality of the refrain, the solo lines of the verse flow smoothly.

> SOLO: *When I went down in the valley to pray*
> CHORUS: *Oh, Rock-a my soul*
> SOLO: *My soul got happy and I stayed all day*
> CHORUS: *Oh, Rock-a my soul.*
>
> CHORUS: (Repeat REFRAIN)

After speaking the verse lines smoothly, ask, "What instrument has that same smooth (legato) quality?" Single children audition this time as the class speaks the lines.

Analyzing Form of Spirituals

Before the children combine instruments and voices, have them study the form of "Rock-a My Soul" which should be written either on the board or on a large chart.

(REFRAIN) CHORUS
(VERSE 1) SOLO, CHORUS, SOLO, CHORUS
(REFRAIN) CHORUS
(VERSE 2) SOLO: *When I was a mourner just like you*
     CHORUS: *Oh, Rock-a my soul*
     SOLO: *I mourned and mourned 'til I come*
           through
     CHORUS: *Oh, Rock-a my soul.*
(REFRAIN) CHORUS

Let the class analyze the spiritual. They will discover that it begins and ends with a refrain which includes everyone (Chorus) and that verses are "sandwiched" in between the refrains. They will also see that a refrain line, *Oh, Rock-a my Soul,* appears in the verse after each of the solo lines. This is the guide for performance.

The class chooses instrumentalists for both the chorus part and the solos. Four different soloists can be chosen for the spoken parts of the two verses. Remind them that their speaking voice should be as musical as the words. Children will want to repeat this performance with different instrumentalists and different soloists. Someone in the class may suggest that instrumentalists play alone between the verses or as an introduction or coda to the speaking. Another time, speaking parts may be performed without percussion or with little percussion to vary the dynamics.

Once into arranging the materials in different ways, children explore various possibilities based on their recognition of the structure.

Other spirituals can be treated in the same way (consult list of source books) and so can many verses in the repertory. This kind of exercise awakens senses to the nuances of language; to the quality of spoken sounds, to dynamics, and voice projection.

There is no *teaching* in the formal sense of the word in collective experiences of this sort. It may surprise a teacher to discover how competent children are both in speaking and in playing instruments when their natural abilities are called into play. They need the *chance* to demonstrate what they can do and congenial materials to work with. One needs only to heighten their awareness of the *quality* of poetry (in this case by comparing the sound to the sound of instruments they know and can play); and of the design in the construction of a poem (the usual *A-B-A* form of spirituals with solo lines of verse followed by a refrain line).

The speech practice involved benefits all the members of a class; repetition necessary to give everyone a chance aids those who need practice but never bores others because of the joy implicit in this combination of modes of expression.

The project gives practice in reading as well, for the class as a whole discovers the form of the spiritual from its written symbols and uses them in planning their performance. No child will be left out on such an occasion for even if he does not immediately recognize the repeated lines he is going to make a great effort to do so in order to have a part in what his classmates are saying and doing. Enthusiasm for the accomplishment is contagious.

Improvising Couplets

Children are drawn to another spiritual, "Hand Me Down," perhaps because the request is phrased in a childlike way.

Hand it down, throw it down. Any way to get it down,
Hand me down my silver trumpet, Lord.

The form of "Hand Me Down," typical of spirituals, is refrain,
verse with solo and chorus voices alternating, and repeat of
refrain. Although the same treatment—with percussion—can
be given this spiritual at some time if the children suggest it,
there are other possibilities to explore.

The poetry of "Hand Me Down" should be written on the
board as below:

> (REFRAIN) CHORUS: *Oh, Hand me down, hand me down,*
> *Hand me down my silver trumpet,*
> *Gabriel.*
> *Hand it down, throw it down, Any*
> *way to get it down*
> *Hand me down my silver trumpet,*
> *Lord.*
>
> (VERSE)   SOLO: *Moses had a lot to do,*
>   CHORUS: *Hand me down my silver trumpet,*
> *Gabriel.*
>   SOLO: *When he led the children of Israel*
> *through*
>   CHORUS: *Hand me down my silver trumpet,*
> *Lord.*
> (REFRAIN repeated as above.)

One way to start children improvising is to substitute for
the standard verse a familiar couplet, as is often done in church
when the leader sees reason to prolong the singing. Write single
lines of these couplets that appear in various spirituals on a
long, narrow piece of cardboard.

> If you get there before I do
> Tell all my friends I'm comin' too.

When I went down to the valley to pray
I got so happy that I stayed all day.

Imitating the "Donkey" game (p. 36), ask for volunteers to
place two single lines of one of the couplets over the lines they
would cover in the original verse. Let the class be the judge of
their success, repeating the process until everyone is sure that
the new solo lines are properly placed. Then go on to solo lines
of the second substitution.

Each try is accompanied by the class reading the verse with
the new line in its proper place. In doing this, they are sensing
the rhythm and length of the poetic phrase.

"Who can make up a new line" is the next question which
the children themselves are likely to ask before the teacher can.
Most children like to work together in a team. An amusing
couplet composed by two boys in one of my classes is

1st solo: *I got a wheel, I split out fas'*
chorus: *Hand me down my silver trumpet, Gabriel.*
2nd solo: *My old feet check out las'*
chorus: *Hand me down my silver trumpet, Lord.*

Maria, who wasn't up to improvising a couplet, but who
still wanted a part in the improvising game, substituted *silver
skates* for *silver trumpet* in the chorus lines. From then on
Gabriel was throwing down all sorts of things: silver bike,
silver cane, golden ring and other objects of wishful thinking.

Several spirituals mention instruments. A favorite one is
"Little David Play on Your Harp."

refrain: *Little David, play on your harp*
Hal-le-loo, Hal-le-loo
Little David, play on your harp
Hal-le-loo.

The gentle-sounding refrain is followed by a verse that
alludes to a dramatic Bible story:

> When David was a shepherd boy
> He slew Goliath and shouted for joy.

Few children can resist the chance to recite their own deeds in this brief form. A change of name and occupation and three words describing the action transform the couplet from a Bible story to a contemporary happening.

Shouts as a Frame

Another kind of religious song is called a *shout*. It is called a shout because the words are chanted with *energy* but not necessarily at a high dynamic level. Originally, the shout was a shuffle-dance which gave form to the continuation of worship outside a church. No instruments were used; the self-made percussive and vocal sounds sufficed to keep the circle of dancers going on into the night.

In the classroom, children are apt to accompany the words with self-made sounds, shuffling or tapping their feet, snapping fingers or clapping on offbeats to establish a firm base for the syncopated rhythm. Any familiar *shout* supplies a model for improvisation of words in this form which is so attractive to children. You might know "Peter Go Ring Them Bells." "Tell John Don't Call the Roll" is printed below. The underscored words are accented by voice emphasis to mark the beats.

VERSE 1: *Tell* John   umph   *don't call* the *roll*
      'Til I   umph   *get there*   *Oh,*
      Tell John   umph   *don't call* the *roll*
      'Til I   umph   *get there*   *Oh,*
      Tell John   umph   *don't call* the *roll*
      'Til I   umph   *get there*   *Oh,*

REFRAIN: *Sinnerman* umph   *you would not believe.*

VERSE 2: *Mary,*   umph   *don't ring* the *bell*
      'Til I   umph   *get there*   *Oh,*
      (repeat 3 times)

REFRAIN: *Sinnerman* umph   *you would not believe.*

VERSE 3:   *Martha,*   umph   *don't draw the line*
           'Til I   umph   *get there*   *Oh,*
                    (repeat 3 times)

REFRAIN: *Sinnerman* umph   *you would not believe.*

VERSE 4:   *Peter,*   umph   *don't bar the gate*
           'Til I   umph   *get there*   *Oh,*
                    (repeat 3 times)

REFRAIN: *Sinnerman* umph   *you would not believe.*

After children have several times chanted a *shout* to their own accompaniment, give them a copy of the words as in verses 2, 3, and 4 above. Let them study it and then write new lines in the frame of the original. A chance for performing their shout with other members of the class as chorus provides an incentive for the effort of making one up.

Improvising in Bilingual Classes

If your class is bilingual, you may want to use the earlier-mentioned Spanish verses and suggested techniques that are appropriate to the sophisticated level of your children.

In addition, there are community music-dance forms that initiate spontaneous versifying. Although not specifically for children, most boys and girls of Latin background are familiar with the kind of response they call forth.

One of the most engaging of these is a Puerto Rican dance the *bomba* that not only initiates versifying but affords creative recreation. It is danced freely in a lively manner to percussive music which is purely instrumental. A description of how adults interpolate speaking in the dance will indicate how it can be enjoyed in a classroom.

Bomba Va!

Bomba Va! is a call given on impulse by an individual during a set of dances. Music and dancing abruptly stop and everyone listens as the caller recites an original four-line verse. The dancers respond with complimentary, satirical, or joking remarks and the music continues until it is interrupted again by *Bomba Va!* The next person to recite a piece may answer the previous one or start on a new tack.

The custom of interrupting music with spoken lines is not unique to Puerto Rico. It is generally practiced in Latin countries, in the Gaucho songs of Argentina, for example, and in *emboladas* of Brazil and Haiti. Spontaneous comments after a soloist's performance—usually jocular—are the rule rather than the exception.

After describing the general idea—or better still, have one of the boys or girls in the class describe it—play a record of Puerto Rican dance music (see Appendix II for Discography). Ask Spanish-speaking children to demonstrate the procedure, speaking a verse they know or improvising a couplet, perhaps, rather than a four-line verse.

To make sure that everyone has a chance to participate within the limit of time scheduled for the Word Lab, suggest that children work in teams during supplementary periods; that they write a rhyme for a spokesman to recite after the call of *Bomba Va!* If five or more spokesmen get a turn in one session, the pleasure of the anticipated activity will spur children to work between times to come up with something witty for the next session. Verses and comments that follow the verses, acceptable in both English and Spanish, brighten the classroom with laughter and gaiety.

Plenas

Another Puerto Rican song-dance-music form is the *plena* in which the lyric is of primary interest. Like *calypso* songs of black culture and *corridos* of Mexican, its lyric is topical, improvised on a subject of interest at the moment. The musical accompaniment is mostly percussive.

According to the Puerto Rican folklorist Francisco López Cruz, the themes of *plenas* cover a wide range of subjects, including topics of current events (he quotes one about the Dempsey-Tunney fight), philosophical comments, religious themes, superstition, humor, love, etc. The essential characteristics of the lyrics are simplicity and repetition.

"Qué Bonita!" and "La Guagua," two folk examples from his book *La Música Folklórica de Puerto Rico*,[2] may strike a sympathetic chord in the ears of Spanish-speaking children. Each of these verses is initiated by a soloist *(Inspirador)* and repeated by a chorus.

The examples are printed here as models for children's improvisations in Spanish, English, or a combination of both. The words are few and phrases are repeated, supplying a simple frame for expressing a subject of class interest. When Spanish-speaking children translate a verse, other members of the class will be eager to try their hand at the form. Many repetitions give those who don't understand Spanish a chance to singsong nonsense syllables to the rhythm until an idea occurs to someone.

In the first example the *Inspirador* chants or recites the whole verse through, which is then repeated by the class. Seeing the Spanish words on the board will help the students execute the rhythm.

The rhythmic structure of the *plena* is a syncopated pattern built on two steady beats to a measure and two measures to a line. In "Qué Bonita!," the syncopation is marked by a

2. Francisco López Cruz, *La Música Folklórica de Puerto Rico* (Sharon, Conn.: Troutman Press, 1967).

silence at the beginning of each of three lines. Beginning these lines with a clap, stamp, grunt, or thrust of the body (on the strong but silent beat marked by an *x*) thrusts the words that follow into place without conscious effort on the part of the reader. Latin children will have no difficulty interpreting this typical Mexican and South American rhythmic pattern. Let them set the example as the class picks up the basic pulse of two beats to a measure by snapping fingers on the first beat and clapping hands on the second. The basic pattern is as below:

1st Measure		2nd Measure	
Snap	Clap	Snap	Clap
x Qué bo-	nita	es!	—
x Qué bo-	nita	es!	—
x Qué bo-	nita	es la mujer que	
Viene de Borin-		quen.	—

When everyone is familiar with the rhythm, help children choose a subject for their own improvisation by suggesting a topic of current interest—something like a campaign slogan for coming elections, the outcome or hoped-for outcome of a school sports event, the locality of a proposed class trip, or anticipated treat, even the name of a classmate.

A *plena* in a slightly different form is "La Gaugua" (The Bus). An *Inspirador* completes the first two lines which are then repeated by the chorus. The rhythmic structure is the same as "Qué Bonita!" but "La Guagua" starts with an upbeat and rolls along just like a bus. Have Spanish-speaking children acquaint others with it as they snap fingers and clap hands as in the other *plena*.

	Snap	Clap	Snap	Clap
Si	quieres go-	zar un	rato ven-	te
Con	migo a la	guagua	—	—

Repeated by chorus

The English translation, "If you want to spend some ·time, come with me on the bus"—in such a jolly rhythm—will start children thinking. Some will want to write their thoughts on paper (in Spanish or English) to work on them a little before they speak them aloud. Allow time for this in the Word Lab period for the suggestion of one child is bound to affect other children's work.

Plenas are an attractive form for children. Ones that may be familiar to bilingual children can be found in the aforementioned *La Música Folklórica de Puerto Rico,* including "Papeles Son Papeles" and "Fuego, Fuego, Fuego." If children are responsive and enthusiastic about this project, it may be further developed in much the same way as described for calypso lyrics in Language Events (p. 154).

Reading Collectively

Children need plenty of exercise in recognizing words and phrases that represent what they know. But there is also a time for boys and girls to discover reading matter on subjects unknown to them. Verses of long ballads are suitable for class exercises not only because of the form but also because there are many to be chosen that interest upper-grade children.

The problem of having a class work together in decoding new material is chiefly one of motivating the less able to make an effort to read without losing the abler students' interest. This can be worked out successfully in Word Lab using the routines of a jazz ensemble as a prototype. As all children know, a sequence of soloists is backed by an accompanying group, each and every one important to the ensemble.

The rhythm of poetry aids the reader as do rhyming words at the ends of lines. In addition the lines are short. Children learn to recite a line of poetry without stumbling from word to word. Folk poetry has these advantages over prose as a teaching tool—and holds greater promise for the least able readers.

In decoding whole words, children should be given clues to track down—clues that intrigue them to investigate further. If the code seems insoluble, especially in the upper grades, boys and girls lose interest in trying to figure it out. In folk poetry, the repetitive lines and words supply clues that motivate children to discover more.

When children work in heterogeneous grouping, the more advanced readers have turns taking the lead with no fanfare about their skill. They help beginners by their *participation in the activity*. The poorer readers are able to go along with the lively experience without feeling ashamed of their particular contribution. A teacher knows when a child is ready to discover a solo line and knows which children in the class need chorus lines as a first step in the process of learning.

Ballads from the black repertory of folk songs make good reading exercises. Each child should be given a complete copy to follow. Since the lyrics of folk songs are in the public domain (unless otherwise noted), they can be reproduced without infringement of copyright laws.

To start the exercise, the teacher gives a short introduction to the ballad to be studied, arousing curiosity by hinting at but not revealing what happens in the text. Every one studies his copy to get a sense of the form and then to discover the chorus lines and, if possible, some solo lines. Children volunteer for the solos in each stanza. Those who feel unequal to tackling a solo keep their place by following the solo lines of the readers in order to come in on their own lines. In following solo lines, a child gains courage to volunteer for a repeated one that "looks like" the one already spoken. Perhaps when the whole ballad is repeated, memory will support eye (if a child is eager rather than frightened) and the last shall become the first to volunteer for a solo.

Humorous Ballads

"Grey Goose" is a ballad useful as an example. After children have been told that a preacher who went hunting on Sunday suffered some crazy consequences, they will want to discover the ridiculous notions that follow one another without ever a letdown. Twenty-four children have a chance at solos the first time through. Some of the solos are alike or so much alike that a hesitant reader will vie for the chance to show his skill.

(SOLO) 1. It was one Sunday morning
Lawd, Lawd, Lawd.
2. The preacher went a-hunting,
Lawd, Lawd, Lawd.

3. He carried along his shotgun,
Lawd, Lawd, Lawd.
4. When along came a grey goose,
Lawd, Lawd, Lawd.

5. The gun went off "Booloo,"
Lawd, Lawd, Lawd.
6. And down came the grey goose,
Lawd, Lawd, Lawd.

7. He was six weeks a-falling,
Lawd, Lawd, Lawd.
8. He was six weeks a-falling,
Lawd, Lawd, Lawd.

9. And my wife and your wife,
Lawd, Lawd, Lawd.
10. They give a feather picking,
Lawd, Lawd, Lawd.

11. They were six weeks a-picking,
Lawd, Lawd, Lawd.

12. And they put him on to par-boil,
    Lawd, Lawd, Lawd.

13. He was six weeks a-boiling,
    Lawd, Lawd, Lawd.
14. And they put him on the table,
    Lawd, Lawd, Lawd.

15. Well, the knife wouldn't cut him,
    Lawd, Lawd, Lawd.
16. And the fork wouldn't stick him,
    Lawd, Lawd, Lawd.

17. They put him in the hog pen,
    Lawd, Lawd, Lawd.
18. And he broke the hog's teeth out,
    Lawd, Lawd, Lawd.

19. They took him to the saw mill,
    Lawd, Lawd, Lawd.
20. And the saw couldn't cut him,
    Lawd, Lawd, Lawd.

21. And the last time I saw him,
    Lawd, Lawd, Lawd.
22. He was flying 'cross the ocean,
    Lawd, Lawd, Lawd.

23. With a long string of goslings,
    Lawd, Lawd, Lawd.
24. And they all going "Quank, Quank."
    Lawd, Lawd, Lawd.

A long ballad that has given children enormous pleasure is the story of the "Boll Weevil." In humorous terms it tells of the misfortunes that befall a cotton farmer. The toughness of the little bug holds children's attention through the nine stanzas.

Because of the repetition of words and phrases and the rhyming words at the end of lines, it is wise to challenge some of the boys and girls who have not been volunteering for solos to make a calculated guess for the first two lines in stanzas 4, 6, and 7. In addition, in this ballad the chorus part varies slightly in repetitions, a form that calls attention to exact wording. Those in the chorus will be helped by following the stanza preceding each chorus which gives the clue, especially in the beginning.

Boll Weevil

1. Oh the boll weevil is a little black bug
    Come from Mexico, they say,
    Come all the way to Texas,
    Just a-looking for a place to stay.

    Just a-looking for a home,
    Just a-looking for a home.

2. The first time I see the boll weevil
    He was sitting on the square.
    Next time I see the boll weevil,
    He had all his family there.

    Just a-looking for a home,
    Just a-looking for a home.

3. The farmer take the boll weevil
    An' he put him in hot sand.
    The boll weevil say "This is mighty hot,
    But, I'll stand it like a man."

    This'll be my home,
    This'll be my home.

4. The farmer take the boll weevil,
    And he put him on a lump of ice.

The weevil say to the farmer,
"This is mighty cool and nice."

This'll be my home,
This'll be my home.

5. The farmer say to the merchant,
"I want some meat and meal."
"Get away from here, you son of a gun,
You got boll weevils in your field."

Going to get your home,
Going to get your home.

6. The farmer say to the merchant,
"We're in an awful fix
The boll weevil ate all the cotton
And left us only sticks."

He'll have our home,
He'll have our home.

7. The farmer say to the merchant,
"We ain't made but only one bale
And before I give you that one,
I'll fight and go to jail."

We'll have a home,
We'll have a home.

8. The merchant got half the cotton,
The boll weevil got the rest,
Didn't leave the farmer's wife,
But one old cotton dress.

And it's full of holes,
And it's full of holes.

9. The farmer say to his missus,
    "Now what you think of that?
    The boll weevil done make a nest
    In my best Sunday hat."

    He's got a home,
    He's got a home.

Ten stanzas of "Old Joe Clark" have plenty of single-syllable words that picture the kind of nonsense children like. Because the ballad is long and also because the stanzas are the funny parts, the chorus part should appear on the board to be spoken only at the beginning, halfway through, and at the end. To vary the treatment, have the class study each stanza with the idea of raising their hands when they know all four lines. Then, call on four children to read a single line, one after the other, preserving the rhythm of the verse. To add interest, have the voices come from different places in the room so that the reading aloud will also be practice in elocution. Once children have read a line, ask them not to raise their hands again until everyone has had a turn at one of the forty lines. The nonsense of the verses will entice even the slow reader to look ahead and find a verse he can read.

Old Joe Clark

CHORUS: *Fare you well, old Joe Clark,*
          Fare you well, I'm gone.
          Fare you well, old Joe Clark,
          Better be getting on.

1. I went up on a mountain top
    To give my horn a blow;
    Thought I heard the preacher say,
    "Yonder comes old Joe."

2. Old Joe Clark had a house
    Was sixteen stories high;

Ev'ry story in that house
Was filled with chicken pie.

3. I went down to old Joe's house,
   Never been there before;
   He slept on a featherbed,
   I slept on the floor.

4. I went down to old Joe's house,
   He was eating supper;
   Stumped my toe on the table leg,
   Stuck my nose in the butter.

5. I went down to old Joe's house,
   He was not at home;
   I ate all of old Joe's meat,
   Left him only the bone.

   (CHORUS)

6. Old Joe had a yellow cat,
   She neither sing nor pray;
   Stuck her head in a buttermilk jar,
   Washed her sins away.

7. Old Joe Clark had a dog,
   Blind as he could be;
   Ran a redbug 'round a stump,
   Racoon up a hollow tree.

8. Old Joe Clark has a cow,
   She was muley born;
   Takes a jay bird forty-eight hours
   To fly from horn to horn.

9. Old Joe Clark has a mule,
   Name is Morgan Brown;
   And every tooth that mule has got
   Is sixteen inches 'round.

10. The higher up the cherry tree,
The riper grows the cherry;
The more you hug and kiss the girls
The sooner they will marry.

(CHORUS)

There is absolutely nothing better than humorous verse
forms from black folklore as material for children to decode as
a class. By taking the pressure off individuals and involving
them in a lively class project, the child who has been unwilling
to risk failure forgets himself and is swept along by class enthusiasm. Nothing succeeds like success. When a child *thinks*
he can read, he wants a try at everything within reach. Having
many collections available on shelves in the classroom—and calling attention to them for perusal in supplementary periods—
surely promotes independent reading.

Humor has an immediate appeal to children but they are
not limited in their responses to this type of material. The poetry
of ballads, spirituals, work chants, community and patriotic
songs—of everything that evokes recognition and response—
are appropriate for collective reading. Verses that children have
interpreted in other media—in wordplay, with percussion,
through dancing and artwork—are then presented as something
to be interpreted by the eye. The association with former experiences gives substance to a reading interpretation.

Legendary Black Heroes

Boys and girls find reading a useful tool when they can read
about adventures of folk heroes like Casey Jones, Railroad Bill,
Long John, and John Henry. Familiarity with the heroes of the
legends and interest in the subject matter hold their attention;
the rhythm of the poetry lightens the task of decoding. Chances
for children discovering the words of such ballads are good even

though the chorus lines may be different after each verse. This is the case in "John Henry."

John Henry

SOLO: 1. *John Henry said to his captain*
             2. *"A man ain't nothing but a man*
             3. *An' before I'll let your steam drill beat me down,*

CHORUS: *Die with the hammer in my hand, Lawd, Lawd,*
                  Die with the hammer in my hand."

SOLO: 4. *John Henry went up to the mountain*
             5. *To beat that steam drill down;*
             6. *John Henry was so small, rock so high,*

CHORUS: *Laid down his hammer an' he died, Lawd, Lawd!*
                  Laid down his hammer an' he died.

SOLO: 7. *John Henry had a little woman*
             8. *Was always dressed in blue;*
             9. *Went down track never looking back,*

CHORUS: *Says, "John Henry, I am true to you, Lawd, Lawd!"*
                  Says, "John Henry, I am true to you."

SOLO: 10. *Who gonna shoe your pretty feet,*
          11. *Who gonna comb your bangs?*
          12. *Who gonna kiss your rose-red lips,*

CHORUS: *Who gonna be your man, Lawd, Lawd!*
                  Who gonna be your man?

SOLO: 13. *Sweet Papa gonna shoe your pretty feet,*
          14. *Sister gonna comb your bangs,*
          15. *Mama gonna kiss your rose-red lips,*

CHORUS: *John Henry gonna be your man, Lawd,*
                 Lawd!
             John Henry gonna be your man.

SOLO: 16. *John Henry had a pretty little woman,*
        17. *Name was Julie Ann;*
        18. *Walked through the lan' with a hammer in*
                 her han'
CHORUS: *Saying, "I drive steel like a man, Lawd,*
                 Lawd!"
             Saying, "I drive steel like a man."

SOLO: 19. *John Henry had a pretty little boy,*
        20. *Sittin' in the palm of his han';*
        21. *He hugged an' kissed and bid him farewell,*
CHORUS: *"Oh son, do the best you can, Lawd, Lawd!*
             Oh son, do the best you can."

As mentioned in connection with work songs, most of the folk verses appear in different versions. Let children understand that this is because the verses are personal expressions of real people who use a theme and vary it as they will. There is no question of a *right* one or a *wrong* one.

To follow up interest in "John Henry," the classroom library should include a children's book, *John Henry: An American Legend,* by Ezra Jack Keats.[3]

Interest in black folk heroes brings up questions of real men who have been heroes for their people. Many books have been published in the last few years which children will enjoy reading independently and discussing with the class. (This subject will be discussed more fully later.) But of the numbers of books available from many different publishers, one should be mentioned here as of particular interest for a class of children of varied reading abilities. It is *The Black BC's* by Lucille Clifton,

3. Ezra Jack Keats, *John Henry: An American Legend* (New York: Pantheon Books, 1965).

beautifully illustrated by Don Miller.[4] The text is a combination of poetry and prose. Each letter of the alphabet is introduced by a capital letter followed by four short lines of poetry that focus on a word starting with the letter.

This is no ordinary ABC book for the kindergartens. The poetry is simple and vigorous, expressing personal convictions and deep feeling. Below the illustration, on each page, ten or twelve lines of prose tell how black people have enriched American life in every field of man's endeavor. The poetry at the top and the illustrations of the book inspire a child to work on the text below, which is written in a simple and frank style to interest people of any age.

Of another type is *What Is Black?*, an attention-getting picture book with two or three lines of text on a page.[5] Its photographs of the contemporary scene appeal to older children as well as young. Poor readers in upper grades, attracted by the photographs, can become involved enough to decode the text.

Choral Speaking

As a climax to a year of enthusiastic reading, a fifth-grade class chose to give a performance of "Lift Ev'ry Voice and Sing" as they arranged it for choral speaking. "Lift Ev'ry Voice and Sing" is an anthem by the poet James Weldon Johnson.

A book of that title [6] was on the shelves of the classroom library. The black-and-white wash drawings by Mozelle Thompson attracted a good deal of attention. Children who thumbed through the book found that the three or four lines of poetry on each page were worth bothering about. Some children knew the poem set to music by Johnson's brother, J. Rosamond Johnson.

4. Lucille Clifton, *The Black BC's* (New York: E. P. Dutton, 1970).
5. Bettye F. Baker, *What Is Black?* (New York: Franklin Watts, 1969). Photographs by Willis Perry II.
6. James Weldon Johnson and J. Rosamond Johnson, *Lift Ev'ry Voice and Sing* (New York: Hawthorn Books, 1970). Illus. by Mozelle Thompson.

There was enough interest in the poem to buy sheet music copies for children to study in pairs.[7] Three groups, each composed of ten children, chose one of the three ten-line stanzas to work on. Although it is not an easy poem to read, boys and girls found the words so stirring that they were willing to expend energy on mastering them. It was not long before they decided to arrange it for choral speaking.

They prepared the program entirely on their own, forming committees to arrange parts for individual and choral speaking. When the preliminary work was done, a rough tryout was held with the whole class taking part. Solo parts were adjusted both as to choice and location of individuals speaking them. Rehearsals ensued; a director was chosen; the performance was ready to be presented!

And an exciting performance it was, one of the most moving I have ever heard. Parents and friends were delighted with the choice of material; teachers and administrators with the quality of performance.

This is the poem they started with:

Lift Ev'ry Voice and Sing

1. Lift ev'ry voice and sing,
   Till earth and heaven ring,
   Ring with the harmonies of Liberty,
   Let our rejoicing rise,
   High as the list'ning skies,
   Let it resound loud as the rolling sea.

   Sing a song full of the faith that the dark past has
       taught us
   Sing a song full of the hope that the present has
       brought us;
   Facing the rising sun of our new day begun,
   Let us march on till victory is won.

7. Sheet music copies of "Lift Ev'ry Voice and Sing" are available from E. B. Marks Music Corp., New York.

2. Stony the road we trod,
    Bitter the chast'ning rod,
    Felt in the days when hope unborn had died:
    Yet with a steady beat,
    Have not our weary feet
    Come to the place for which our fathers sighed?

    We have come over a way that with tears has been
        watered,
    We have come treading our path thro' the blood of
        the slaughtered,
    Out from the gloomy past, till now we stand at last
    Where the white gleam of our bright star is cast.

3. God of our weary years,
    God of our silent tears,
    Thou who hast brought us thus far on the way;
    Thou who hast by Thy might
    Led us into the light,
    Keep us forever in the path, we pray.

    Lest our feet stray from the places, our God, where
        we met Thee,
    Lest our hearts, drunk with the wine of the world,
        we forget Thee;
    Shadowed beneath Thy hand, may we forever stand,
    True to our God, true to our native land.

When children's sensibilities are aroused, it is surprising to see how well they cope with something normally considered beyond their ability. But they need to have their heart in the task which, however difficult, then becomes transformed to *play*.

Successive repetitions of oral experiences in every grade with higher levels of sophistication and profundity induce the kind of learning which leads to mastery of elementary skills.

Exploring Reading Materials

What You Hear Is What You Read

5

As we have seen, lyric verses from black and Hispanic folklore provide dynamic material for varied exercises that all children in a class take part in together. Folklore in prose from these cultures can achieve the same results. But, like folk poetry, prose writings hold greater promise of engaging every child's attention if they are animated by various classroom activities. The content and style of the prose are suitable for this treatment. Not only is prose folklore within the grasp of the child who can read, but it furnishes motivation in a positive way for other children to gain the skill.

Reading to Children

An abundance of material is available but children cannot be expected to explore the richness and variety of the literature on their own. Reading aloud to an entire class allows every child to participate in the enjoyment that books afford. Building on their responses in various ways to be described sends children to the books because they want and need to refine their impressions in order to achieve a specific goal. Providing a variety of books and specifying times to browse through them get children used to handling books, examining their content, and little by little taking steps to decode the print.

Aside from other benefits derived, a practical reason for reading aloud to children of other cultures is to implant the sound of standard English on attentive ears. What children hear at such a time makes a profound impression on them. When storytelling time is a happy event that occurs daily in the classroom, children unconsciously adopt school expressions in discussions and reenactment of the stories.

Slow Learners

Even a nonreader can become accustomed to using books. For example, a question that arises may be clarified by an illustration as well as by print. Or a child, thumbing through a book, may come upon intriguing illustrations and ask that the story be read aloud by the teacher. Children become venturesome as they explore books if they are confident that they will not be embarrassed or ridiculed.

Poor readers of any age start by looking at pictures and title words which lead them to discover familiar characters and the thread of a story line. If their own incentive is great enough, they begin to recognize more—a repeated phrase they have heard, a short sentence that has been used in a class dramatization, a bit of conversation which has been mimicked in the classroom and seen written on the board. In this way, visual and aural memory—bolstered constantly by phonics and an organized course of study—is exercised by recognizing whole words and phrases that have had functional use in serious play. As confidence grows, a child secretly tackles a longer passage. If he succeeds, he is on his way to reading. If he fails, he can either seek help from a teacher or a classmate or keep his secret as well as his courage to try again. When children are properly motivated by involvement with subject matter, they make the effort it takes to discover in print whatever is necessary to reach a chosen objective.

Classroom Activities

Various classroom activities, similar to those described for verse forms, develop from work with folklore in prose. They can be summarized as follows:

Young children:
    Participate in the telling of a story
    Talk about a story after it is read
    Retell incidents
    Act out incidents of one or more episodes
    Make a book, writing either one episode or a complete story
    Make up a story, using the form of a folk tale as a model
    Use art media in various ways
    Make puppets and put on a puppet show
    Make up dances and/or music for a play

Older children can do all the above plus the following:

Independently research a subject for cooperative projects

Communicate ideas to others through various media

Make a map, on which the names of places are followed by the name of a fable from that country

Engage in rap sessions to derive figurative meaning of fables

Recast a theme in a contemporary setting to develop an original story or play

Plan and execute a TV show with original folk-tale material or with the theme updated

Third World Stories

The cultural fountainhead of storytelling is Africa. African story material translated in English can be found in several collections.[1] Many Latin-American tales are also translated into English, usually interspersed with Spanish words with a glossary and guide to pronunciation at the back of the books.[2] Some stories are printed with both English and Spanish text.

Stories told by English-speaking people of the West Indies,[3] as well as stories from the southern United States,[4] are plentiful. Some contemporary folklorists try to preserve the rhythm and spirit of the original storytellers' speech in colloquial language that is easy to read and understand. In fact, many such stories are an easy-to-cross bridge between dialect and standard English. The sound of them read aloud has a familiar ring which acts as a magnet to draw children into a circle of listeners.

1. For African fables, see annotated listing in Bibliography.
2. For Latin-American tales, see annotated listings in Bibliography under locality: General, Puerto Rican, Mexican.
3. For West Indies fables and stories in English, see annotated listing in Bibliography.
4. For stories from southern United States, see annotated listings in Bibliography.

On the other hand, the *Uncle Remus* stories by Joel Chandler Harris, although authentic folk tales, defeat the objectives of reading aloud. The style of writing is a poor approximation of black speech popularized in minstrel shows. Fortunately many of the same stories appear in other collections.

Fables for Primary Grades

Of all the folk tales in the oral tradition, fables take first place. They are the major prose creation of Africans and their descendants and have retained their vitality in both Afro-American and Afro-Antillean cultures.

Because fables are the prototype of storytelling, they will be dealt with extensively here. But other folk tales and modern stories in the tradition—many of which show the influence of fables—lend themselves to similar treatment in the classroom.

If the reader questions the appropriateness of fables for urban children, let me point out that a good story on any subject is fascinating to all children, and that fables tend to be particularly meaningful to black and Latin children as part of their heritage.

All children identify with creatures of nature and read into their actions traits of human behavior. They naturally ally with creatures who are small and weak as they are apt to see themselves in relation to the powerful grown-ups they encounter every day. Stories that combine fact and fancy have a special appeal for white and black children alike. Some of the best-loved stories in the Euro-American tradition use the same devices as fables. Their very charm lies in the fanciful characters and settings. An endless number of examples illustrate: E. B. White's *Charlotte's Web, Stewart Little,* and *Trumpeter's Swan; Winnie the Pooh* and his friends in that series of books; Mole, Toad, and company in *Wind and the Willows;* the classic Alice who meets many strange creatures in Wonderland; Mickey and Minnie

Mouse of Disney fame; the comic strip *Peanuts* and innumerable puppets and cartoon characters that children see on television.

Participatory Listening

Fables are simply told and easy to understand; the language reflects children's speech. The stories are told with much conversation and a minimum of descriptive narrative. Stock characters, bearing human traits, reappear again and again.

The sentence structure is succinct and precise. In many stories, episodes are repeated with slight variations, often duplicating conversation and actions set forth in the first episode. Their construction is like the musical form of theme and variation. The theme is set forth in the first episode and varied in succeeding episodes (which can be added ad infinitum) by change of one of the characters or locality. This allows children to anticipate the story and actually take part in telling it. They also join in on a repeated line, singsonging it into a refrain.

Children show their involvement in many ways, sometimes by underscoring the action, with cheers for clever Brer Rabbit, and boos for his opponents. In one story, Wolf is scared away by Brer Rabbit's show of strength. He sees Brer Rabbit "beating" Elephant. The children are delighted because they know that Brer Rabbit offered to scratch Elephant's back in order to fool Wolf.

Children intuitively understand that fables combine fact and fancy, squealing with delight to hear the boasting, the enormous exaggerations, the easily recognized twisting of fact, and the unctuous flattery of a rival in order to cause his downfall.

Hearing and Seeing

As children relate to the symbolic stories, they learn to observe realistic details that are intrinsic to the plot and appear in the book's illustrations. Many stories revolve around distinctive characteristics of beasts and insects: how Rabbit lost his tail; why Zebra has stripes; how animals got furry coats; why Spider's waist is thin; and a host of other physical features. Fables also explain the beginnings of things in a childlike way, increasing awareness of natural phenomena through fanciful stories about why Moon changes shape every night; why Thunder went to the Skies; why the elements of Fire, Water, Rain, Darkness, and Light, each personalized, behave as they do.

The stories, full of the kind of humor children love, can open eyes to the wonders of the world; can open ears to simplicity of precise language; can open minds to infinite possibilities of the imagination.

Thus can fables be used to forward the development of auditory and visual faculties, refining a child's sense of hearing and seeing. They can aid a child in making a transferral from active participation in the enjoyment of the stories to the printed page on which they are represented. For children are drawn to the books that house the fables, to look at pictures of their favorite characters and to find the stories they want to hear again, or to choose an unfamiliar one with interesting pictures or with conversation they discover as familiar.

In time, first one child and then another will recognize words here and there and together make the effort to piece out the story by recalling other bits they remember hearing. They help each other but also do not hesitate to seek help from a teacher who leads them to associate sound with symbol.

Social Customs

Fables reflect the mores of the society that creates them. Not all fables point to a moral but they all picture attitudes and customs. Friendship is highly valued among the creatures of the forest and visits are regularly exchanged. Food or drink is offered and served and manners are observed in consuming the offerings. One comes to the table clean and eats with or without a jacket as local custom dictates.

The themes cover a wide gamut of subjects, sometimes with a trickster figure as the hero. But even in those stories that center on a trick played on a rival, the trick is of a mild nature, unlike the physical violence so typical in cartoons. A trick is cleverly planned to gain an objective, such as effecting an escape from capture, outwitting an opponent to get food, winning a contest, redressing an injustice, or setting right false gossip.

The prevailing mood in the community of nature's creatures is that members work together for the common good and help a friend in trouble. Everyone enjoys parties together, entertaining each other with stories, song, dance, and instrumental music.

Polite Greetings

One aspect of traditional customs still practiced today in black communities is evidenced in the formality of ordinary social greetings. "Live long, may years be added to your years" is a current example.[5]

Many African fables begin with this kind of polite concern for the well being of all members of the family.

"Good day to you, Lion."

"Good day to you, Hare."

"Have you slept well, Lion?"

"Yes, Hare, I have slept well."

"And your wife, Lion, has she slept well?"

"Yes, Hare, my wife has slept well."

"And your children, Lion, have they also slept well?"

"Yes, Hare, and my children also."

5. *An African Treasury*, selected by Langston Hughes. Articles/Essays/Stories/Poems by Black Africans (New York: Pyramid Books, 1960). Paperback.

Children are quick to pick up such formalities and take pleasure in mimicking the animals' greetings in the classroom.

Writing lines like the above in various spots on the board *out* of sequence and asking the class as a whole to put them in proper order, either orally or in their notebooks, gives a teacher an opportunity to use the greetings as a reading and writing game.

Another convention that lends itself to associating sound and sight comes from Jamaica. When listeners are assembled, the story begins with two lines of dialogue:

> Crick crack   *(said by storyteller)*
> Break my back   *(response by listeners)*

The story is ended:

> Wire bend   *(said by storyteller)*
> Story end   *(response by listeners)*

Children often begin and end the stories they write with these words. And when they apply they can be used as sound-and-sight references for decoding other words.

Acting Out Episodes

When children hear many fables, enjoy working with their words and sentences, and feel part of the ambience the stories create, they want to act out a favorite one. Because they have participated in the telling of stories, they are familiar with the usual form in which conversation and action are repeated with a change of character in a series of short episodes. A general outline of an African fable will illustrate how the theme and variation form allows for important contributions from every member of a class.

The original impetus for dramatizing is given in Word Lab by reading the story aloud. Teams are then formed to work out particular episodes and a script of that episode is given them. Teamwork is carried out in supplementary periods and then the result of their efforts is brought back into the Lab. Each child in a team learns from his or her peers and teaches them in turn in all aspects of the project. They need little or no help in devising movements or accompaniment for the part they have chosen to do.

A common setting for many fables is the waterhole, an essential gathering place for all creatures of the neighborhood. In this fable, the waterhole has dried up; the story tells *How the Animals Dug a Well*.[6]

The scene is set with a series of short sentences which would be spoken by different members of one team.

> The earth was dry.
> No rain fell.
> Streams dried up.
> Rivers dried up.
> Plants dried up and died for lack of water.
> Still no rain fell.
>
> So Lion, king of all the animals,
> Called together
> Chiefs of other animals.

Lion's command is the *refrain* which, written on the board, may be repeated by the entire class before and after each episode.

> We must dig a well.
> Each must do his share.
> Dig a deep, deep well.

6. *How the Animals Dug a Well—Making Music Your Own*, Book 3 (Morristown, N.J.: Silver Burdett, 1971).

Each must do his share.
Dig a deep, deep well.

One member of the first team says: *The sound of drumming was heard all over the land*, which is followed by drumming and voices as the families of animals assemble:

Oh, we must dig a well!
Dig a deep, deep well!

The following episodes, repeated for each type of animal, are
pantomimed by different teams to describe how the well was
dug: Lion is first, calls for his drummers and his helpers, and
begins to dance. One or more members of the Lion team says:

He danced and danced
He kicked up the dry earth
In a circle on the ground.

When Lion grew tired, he said
"See I have started the well.
Come, Sir Monkey, I give my place to you.
Dig!"

After Sir Monkey's team repeats the action and narrative,
Sir Buffalo's family has a turn, dancing with heavy feet. Then
Sir Giraffe's family in a gallop. As many more episodes can
be added as children have suggestions for animals whose size
and style of movement they know.
    The last episode is one of rejoicing, the first part spoken
by one child, the second part by all the class.

So each animal did his share of digging.
The well became deeper and deeper.
Suddenly, water gushed forth.

The well has water!
The well has water!
Let us rejoice.
There is water to drink.

Like folk verses, the form calls for individual and group improvisations in mime, dancing, and drumming for any number of episodes. The form supplies a theme and a structure as the impetus and shape for creative activity.

Thus a rewarding experience for every one in the class results from the simple beginning of reading a fable. You can rely on children to develop their ideas in accord with their own drives. The teacher's part is mainly to introduce the material in Word Lab; to give children time to work with it in teams (the abler helping the less able) in supplementary period; and to make sure that the practice of academic skills in reading and writing are an integral part of the creative activity.

Making Up a Story

The structure of fables—terse sentences, short episodes duplicated with slight variations—serves as a model for making up a story in class. Have children talk about the setting for their story—a particular block in the city or suburbs, the inside of an apartment, the front stoop or firehouse. When as many ideas have been entertained as are forthcoming, take a vote to decide the locality. Then what shall be the theme? The children's words to locate the setting or the theme may well supply a line or two for a refrain. This should be written on the board and chanted by the children until someone is clamoring to suggest the first episode.

The story that is built, episode after episode, first collectively in Word Lab and then refined in writing by teams working on each episode, will likely have some characteristics of its African prototype. For when children know all the details of their setting there is no need for superfluous details; every allusion is readily understood by members of a class. The story will be succinctly told in their own language, embellished only by their own imaginations and, hopefully, self-made music and dance.

Folk Tales for the Upper Grades

In the upper grades, students can penetrate beneath the surface of incidents to get at the deeper meaning of folk tales. Arna Bontemps points out that the folk tales of the Negro slaves were projections of personal experiences, of their hopes and defeats. In the fables, Brer Rabbit became the hero because he is the most frightened and helpless creature. But through his cleverness, he defeated powerful Brer Wolf, stupid Brer Bear, sly Brer Fox. Digging for deeper meanings adds interest to simple stories which are useful in the classroom as reading material to accommodate a range of abilities.

Not all stories, however, are about creatures or natural phenomena. In some African fables, kings, queens, princesses, as well as local farmers, intermingle with creatures of the forest or carry the story alone. In the southern United States, there are stories about John and the Boss, plantation slaves and masters, farmwork and crops. A famous fable from Puerto Rico is about a witch who holds a boy captive until he guesses her name (a not unusual theme in folklore). Poor Juan Bobo, always in trouble, is a human character in Puerto Rican stories, as are Malice and Boqui in Haiti and other Creolean islands. In Mexico, Indian legends allude to historical events (part true, part legendary) and other tales in Mexico bear a strong resemblance to their African prototype.

The style of storytelling is always allegorical, challenging conceptual thinking. Although the setting of the tales and the characters who take part in them rarely appear in children's physical environment, boys and girls are able to perceive that like actions happen every day; that strengths and weaknesses of the creatures represent universal traits of character. These are subjects to discuss in class to help children think conceptually.

Widening Knowledge of Third World

In the process of study, boys and girls become aware that environment influences the choice of creatures in folk tales and affects customs and values. The big animals in African stories, for example—Lion, Leopard, Tiger, Elephant—do not appear in tales from the West Indies or the southern United States. Each country features indigenous creatures, and occupations and customs that are particularly characteristic of the locale.

Many collections of fables have texts describing the life and work of people who live in the region where the stories are told. Thus a reading project extends into the field of geography and social studies, with by-products of dance, drama, artwork, and music.

An interest in other people and the nature of their land can lead to making a map, pinpointing the place of origin of particular stories. Then groups of children choose a country's folklore to investigate on their own—from Africa, English-French-Spanish West Indies, southern United States, or Mexico (the latter doubly endowed with both Indian and African folk tales).

While some of the children in a single class are reading independently, others are still searching for a foothold. But each child makes a contribution in a cooperative research project according to his particular strength. Children stimulate each other and keep interest alive. A watchful teacher creates opportunities for change of leadership in a multi-media endeavor and each child comes to value what can be gained from books through successful participation in interpreting content.

When groups pool their experiences in class reports, they

make another discovery: that although each country's lore has distinctive features, certain themes are recurrent, appearing in several places with slight variations.

Recurrent Themes

The story of the race between Tortoise and Hare, well known as an Aesop fable, turns up in African lore as well as in that of other localities. In Mexico the race is run by Rabbit and Frog with Frog's family tricking the boastful Rabbit. Other recurrent themes can be summarized as follows:

Tales about sharing the crops are told with human characters in the United States; with animal characters in Africa.

Guessing secret names is a theme worked out with different incidents in African, Puerto Rican, and North American lore.

How creatures flatter their captors to gain release is the subject of tales in Africa, Puerto Rico, and the United States.

How captive creatures, in order to escape, divert their masters by singing, dancing, or drumming is a favorite theme in Africa, in Puerto Rico and other islands of the West Indies, and also in the States.

Why the turtle's back is cracked is told with different incidents in various localities.

Finding a suitable mate is a recurrent theme which has an ant as protagonist in one tale in Puerto Rico and a cockroach in another, and in Africa, a white mouse. In addition there are many tales of suitors, man or beast, performing miraculous deeds to win the hand of a princess.

Anansi, the spider or spider-man turns up everywhere.

He is so popular that stories in the South used to be called Anansi-tales. The American Anansi is known as Ananse in Africa. A favorite fable in Ghana is about a wax dummy who was set in a field to catch Ananse. A 16-mm. film, *No Tears for Ananse*, was made of the fable by a Ghana film unit. A print of it is available from the Ghana Embassy in Washington, D.C.

The sticky gum figure who captures garden thieves, (wax dummy in Africa, *Tar Baby* in the United States) is found wherever fables are told.

Children are truly excited when they hear a theme they know reported by a classmate who has been studying another part of the world. They exchange notes and vie with each other for the authenticity of their version.

"Mine is the *real* story," says José. "No, mine is," says Dolores. No matter; they are defending their research as scholars do. And their minds are stimulated by its rewards.

A Source Book

Along with the continuing pleasure of listening to stories read aloud, of studying the association between what is heard and what is seen in printed symbols, and of interpreting favorite tales in various ways, each member of the class should be scheduled with a partner for the privilege of spending time looking at a most thorough and inspiring book called *African Folk Tales and Sculpture.*[7] This book is a *must* for every school library.

There are two sections in this big and beautiful book; the first is devoted to the retelling of traditional folk tales, and

7. *African Folk Tales and Sculpture*, selected and edited by Paul Radin and Elinore Marvel (New York: Pantheon Books, Bollinger Series XXXII, 1952). Sculpture selected by James Johnson Sweeney.

the second contains pages and pages of photographs of African sculpture and artifacts. Children of any age can fill time pleasurably by looking at these wonderful works of art. Inevitably, as a consequence of interest, they thumb through the first section of printed stories to find a familiar one.

In the Introduction to the sculpture section, James Johnson Sweeney writes:

> . . . it is not the tribal characteristics of Negro Art nor its strangeness that are interesting. It is the sculptural quality—its vitality of forms, its simplification without impoverishment, its consistent three-dimensional organization of structural planes . . . and above all its uncompromising truth to material.

The artifacts of wood, used alone or in combination with other materials, natural, whitened or painted in polychrome, are wonderful to behold. There are photographs of four-faced masks in the form of a helmet, some with raffia beards, cloth or hair, details decorated with shells; or freestanding figures of various types—equestrian, mother and child, ancestor figure (which resembles somewhat a pilgrim father)—of seated figures with drums, some with bowls, one woman with a raffia skirt; and other figures that serve as chief's stool, as seats and benches, or, in smaller forms, as details of other useful objects. There are also spoons, musical instruments made of wood with finely detailed handles, gong hammers, gourds, batons, etcetera.

The African's respect for materials—which he believed to be imbued with a spirit—shows through all the sculpture. Gold, bronze, hammered brass, iron, copper, ivory, soapstone, and terra cotta are handled with great sensibility to their natural properties.

Looking at the photographs in this book initiates various projects of both a creative and academic nature, as well as instills an enormous respect for African culture. African masks, as one instance, motivate children to interpret their own ideas in a similar way.

An exhibition recently held in New York's Natural History Museum showed artwork created by children from Intermediate School 201. Masks, wood carvings, linoprints, and paintings of remarkable beauty and invention came out of a classroom study of African and Afro-American culture. Research in books, visits to the museum, and listening to recordings were all part of the intensive twelve-week study that inspired the children's work.

Developing and Reinforcing Skills

Learning to read need not be a lonely or laborious job. With sufficient motivation, it can be an adventure, full of exciting and fascinating challenges. When children enjoy sharing what they learn and taking part in what their peers learn, they find reason and purpose in discovering what is inside the covers of a book.

Skills develop as productive experiences are backed by organized study of techniques. A comprehensive approach to reading instruction balances output with input, giving children the tools to accomplish what seems to them a desirable objective. One kind of learning reinforces the other; neither is completely effective alone.

The greater is the variety of reading materials to offer children, the greater is the chance of reaching every one in some way. Materials used for reading must command children's respect, hold their interest, and be simple enough technically for the less able to grapple with. Another classification in folklore that meets these specifications is the proverb or aphorism, a short allegorical statement in prose.

Proverbs

Every language has its share of these pithy expressions of wisdom. In African and Afro-American society, proverbs are quoted in many situations—in the home, at work, in social gatherings, and, because they are widely known, as material for the talking drum.

A collection entitled *African Proverbs*, compiled by Charlotte and Wolf Leslau gathers together proverbs from many parts of the continent.[8] It is a treasurehouse which can furnish reading material for years on end.

The first proverb in the book is Ashanti. It reads:

Rain beats a leopard's skin,
But it does not wash out the spots.

When children are acquainted with the appearance of a leopard from pictures illustrating a folk tale or from a visit to the zoo, the obvious truth of the saying strikes them instantly. To help them dig deeper into the meaning of the metaphor (and to promote skills of reading and verbalizing) the Ashanti proverb is written on the board above an English one and children are asked how they are alike.

Sticks and stones will break my bones
But names will never hurt me.

A favorite character in fables as well as in the zoo is the monkey. He appears in many proverbs. Two from Cameroon proverbs, easy to understand, get children thinking and talking:

Do not dispose of the monkey's tail
before he is dead.

By trying often, the monkey learns to
jump from the tree.

Some children may know the English proverb that relates to the monkey jumping from the tree:

8. *African Proverbs*, compiled by Charlotte and Wolf Leslau (Mount Vernon, N.Y.: Peter Pauper Press, 1962).

> If at first you don't succeed,
> Try, try again.

Another one on the same theme is from the Congo:

> Little by little grow the bananas.

Introduce Euro-American proverbs and aphorisms which all children are likely to be familiar with.

> Where there is a will
> There is a way.

> Don't cry over spilled milk.

> A stitch in time
> Saves nine.

It may surprise a teacher to discover how often such sayings are used in everyone's conversation without conscious thought of searching for an explicit metaphor. Once awakened to this idea, share with the children any you find yourself using.

In fact, proverbs or aphorisms are so well known by people in general that in modern usage one often gives only the first line, implying the second. In speaking about troubles piling up, it is not unusual to say: *It never rains* implying *but it pours.*

This brings to mind a writing exercise for children. When they know many proverbs, give only the first line either in voice, written on the board or on a strip of cardboard. Ask them to write the remaining line in their notebooks. Or, as a reading exercise, have them match the beginnings of metaphors in a left-hand column and the ends jumbled in a right-hand column.

Calling on Grown-Ups at Home

Some children might want to copy aphorisms from the *Book of Negro Folklore* [9] to show to adult relatives or friends, who, in turn, will be reminded of other aphorisms. Encourage children to talk to people about these meaty sayings, quoting those they work with at school to introduce the subject. Spanish-speaking parents may know the equivalent of:

> A bird in the hand is
> Worth two in the bush.

Frances Toor in *A Treasury of Mexican Folkways* [10] gives the above as the English equivalent for:

> Más vale pájaro en mano
> Que cien volando.

Literally: *A bird in the hand is worth more than a hundred flying.*

The literal meaning of this proverb can be conveyed in actions as well as words. Were this one and another (such as, *Don't count your chickens before they are hatched*) written on the board, it would be a challenge to the class to discover which of the two a child was acting out. Such a game activity brings words to life and helps all members of a class realize the significance in verbal expression: for once the words are recognized, conversation about meaning is bound to follow. Most every child feels he/she would rather have a dime in the pocket now than a promise of fifty cents two weeks hence.

Other Spanish proverbs are quoted in *Mexican Folkways* with comparable meaning and literal translations in English.

---

9. *The Book of Negro Folklore*, ed. Langston Hughes and Arna Bontemps (New York: Dodd, Mead, 1958).
10. Frances Toor, *A Treasury of Mexican Folkways* (New York: Crown Publishers, 1947).

Because of the short form, proverbs are easy to read but they provoke thoughtful reading and get children to use many words in English to convey their meaning. A project of collecting proverbs from grown-ups, Spanish- or English-speaking, might well give children the impetus to write (from the adults' dictation), to explain the meaning of a concise statement in words or actions (by sharing a proverb with their peers), and to take an interest in verbal expression itself (in recognizing the use of methaphor in this short form). Most of the folk anthologies [11] besides the two mentioned include innumerable witty sayings of this type to supply abundant material for classroom use.

Talking Drums

But language is not the only way of communicating in African societies. An expert drummer conveys the sound of a particular proverb, saying, or poem on a "talking" drum. Because of the predominance of open vowel sounds in African languages, a drummer can manipulate the various tonal qualities of a drum to *approximate* the sound of a phrase, adapting his interpretation to the tempo, rhythm, dynamics of sound sequences and to the style of the whole. The listener in order to understand must, of course, be familiar with the category from which a particular selection is chosen. Because the drum does not speak a precise language, the subject or idea interpreted must be known both to the sender of the message and the receiver.

The principle underlying the talking drum is applicable in the classroom. It is an *aural* symbol for speech just as print is a visual symbol. A reason for introducing the drum is to use every device possible to catch the interest of children in the sound and meaning of words. To combine the visual and audi-

11. For anthologies of folklore, see annotated listing in Bibliography.

tory faculties, write three proverbs on the board. Ask a child to choose one of the three (but don't tell which) and interpret it on a drum for others to guess. Children listen intently to discover what the drum is saying and can scarcely wait for their turn as drummer.

The performer may catch the *spirit* of the proverb or he may tap out the syllables of the words. This brings up a nice difference between guessing a *literal* rendition of words from its rhythmic pattern on a drum and guessing it from an interpretation of its meaning. Certainly the latter way calls for greater sensibility and perception and focusses on the *meaning* of words. The former focuses on the rhythm of syllables. But both ways are fascinating to children and achieve the desired end of involving them with words and their meaning.

Reading Independently

Contemporary Literature: Poetry and Prose

6

After the first overtures toward books made expressly for the purpose of contributing to a collective experience, there comes a time in a child's development when the many fragments of learning must be pieced together into a realization that he/she can read independently. At such a time, the nature of available reading matter is of utmost concern. The printed page must appear simple enough to promise success in decoding and yet embody ideas sufficiently intriguing to be worthy of the effort decoding demands.

It has been my experience in working with upper-grade boys and girls that to motivate reading independently greater consideration must be given to chronological age than to achievement level; that any hint of condescension implied in the nature of subject matter offered for suggested or required reading turns children off instantly. Youngsters grow up fast in this society, and upper-grade boys and girls have a knowledge of life far beyond those of the same age a few decades ago. No matter what their scholastic standing is, life experience adds years to their maturity. For this reason, young readers are more likely to achieve success in independent reading when subject matter is appropriate to their years.

All children appreciate being viewed as growing *people*, capable of making choices and judgments. The child who has been slow in learning skills of reading especially needs to gain the confidence that comes from accomplishment on a level respected by peers. Sharing the fruits of individual labor with members of a class in a supportive environment bolsters the ego of any child and furnishes the motivation for continuing effort to practice the skill of reading.

Word Lab in the upper grades can then become a clearing house for the exchange of ideas gleaned from independent reading. Children individually or in teams read aloud the short pieces they have chosen to work on in supplementary periods; new pieces are introduced by the teacher. A story or poem, well received, circulates widely through the class. Interaction and interchange of ideas on interpretation of reading materials keeps interest high and constantly stimulates further research.

Children's graded books for independent reading will be discussed later in this chapter, but along with books of graded reading, an upper-grade classroom should afford children at every stage of development the opportunity to discover ungraded materials that have strong appeal for them and through which they can gain some measure of success in acquiring techniques of reading.

Ungraded Anthologies [1]

Anthologies of contemporary literature representative of Afro-American and Afro-Antillean cultures meet the need for ungraded materials in a most practical way. Those of contemporary literature, devoted to a single subject, contain selections of work by one or more writers of poetry, stories, historical essays, biographies, or important speeches. Others compiled by folklorists who are interested in ethnic cultures as they are practiced today can be considered contemporary folklore. They contain the words of living people just as they were spoken in the normal course of the day. They include poems in the folk manner, wise sayings, stories, accounts of happenings, and other types of interesting narratives.

Ungraded anthologies furnish valuable material for children to use in independent reading. The selections include many different styles of writing, giving opportunity to slower readers to choose those which appear simple in print: few words on a line, some recognizable words in title or first paragraph, and familiar words to use as clues for discovering the general idea of the subject. The effort then of phonetically decoding other words either independently or with the help of a teacher seems worthwhile.

Well-chosen selections of contemporary works by ethnic writers reach children in the upper grades. Subject matter is, in general, concerned with things they think about. The literature has substance as well as a directness in expression comprehensible to boys and girls. Motivation for deciphering a chosen piece is intensified when children can look forward to reciting it in Word Lab as an example of their own choosing.

The enormous variety that all anthologies include in their chosen subjects (whether it be a collection of poetry or prose)

---

1. For anthologies of contemporary literature, folklore, and children's original poetry see annotated listing in Bibliography.

increases the possibility of catching the eye of every child in the class. This is the particular value in making anthologies available to children.

Introducing Reading Materials

In exercising his/her judgment and taste in choosing pieces to read aloud, a teacher works up enthusiasm for the material that is inevitably communicated to children. It has been proved time and again that children's work is favorably affected by a teacher's enthusiasm for the subject being taught.

The material a teacher chooses to read is, of course, a personal matter. In my own work, I tend to select those things that highlight traditional values of the culture and underplay the subjective writings of the angry or disheartened. The reason for this choice is simple: children of minority groups need to develop a positive self-image. Many children are already overburdened by the circumstances of their birth and identifying with the positive values of their culture gives them a solid base for self-esteem. To become absorbed with aesthetic pleasures that *objectively* relate to one's existence buoys up the spirit and releases a child, even if temporarily, from internal and external cares.

At the same time, choices that children make on their own from anthologies of ungraded poems and stories should never be disregarded or censored in actuality or by implication. It is a mistake to shy away from serious topics, to cut short an impassioned discussion. Children make strides in personality development when they express deep feelings and give voice to inner thoughts.

In order to involve all members of an upper-grade class in the reading of contemporary literature, children should be introduced to a great variety of short pieces. A teacher might start by reading aloud several selections over a period of days to test children's reactions. What subjects cause a stir in the classroom, catch the attention of the least responsive students? What topics promote discussion? What type of narrative is open-ended in that it allows flexibility for individual or class interpretations?

After several selections are read aloud, children will have a basis for voicing preferences. The type of literature they choose to study and the way they go about it will undoubtedly be an individual matter. Some children proceed cautiously, asking that a favorite piece be reread before they attempt to discover it in print; the more venturesome turn to the book their choice came from to try independently to find something else of a similar type. Some children will work alone; others will feel more secure contributing their efforts in a study group. But each will find his way, for when children are stimulated by ideas—ideas they have tossed about in class discussions—they gain incentive to seek further for reading matter that can be shared with classmates.

Serendipity plays a role. In thinking through a book, a child may recognize a few words that were read aloud in class. Or she/he may come upon a provocative title or picture that arouses enough interest to work at discovering the subject matter it denotes. Sometimes children will be attracted to a general category in a Table of Contents of a collection and become absorbed in decoding the titles of various chapters. Consider, for example, the enticement of such chapter headings as "The Jazz Folk," "Harlem Jive," and "Ghost Stories" to mention only a few to be found in *The Book of Negro Folklore*.[2]

One step leads to another. If the heading of a particular category strikes the fancy, a boy or girl is impelled to investigate its contents and may ask a teacher to read aloud what he or she is unable to decipher.

2. *The Book of Negro Folklore*, ed. Langston Hughes and Arna Bontemps (New York: Dodd, Mead, 1968).

Contemporary Poetry

Children who are learning to read are apt to be drawn to poetry, for its short lines offer greater chance of immediate success than longer sentences and paragraphs typical of the essay style of writing. Once a child gains proficiency in a short-lined form, however, she or he will have no difficulty in applying the same techniques in deciphering any style of writing. Since poetry has been a popular vehicle for expressing ideas among Afro-American writers from Washington's day to the present, the style has influenced contemporary works of many black- and Latin-American writers.[3] Selections in poetic style not only appear simpler on the page and actually are easier to decipher, but they lend themselves to an experiential interpretation which involves many children in the process of reading independently.

Reading with Musical Accompaniment

A team project for a few children is to study a poem together, planning that it be read aloud in Word Lab with musical accompaniment. Reading with a musical background adds importance to a "language event," giving incentive to study and, incidentally, improving a child's delivery. For such an occasion, the accompaniment would be interpretive of the spirit of the work rather than a literal tapping out of syllables of words.

Although a teacher might hesitate to improvise an accompaniment for a reading, the child who chooses to do so will approach the task with confidence. Boys and girls need no specific musical directions to improvise an accompaniment; they need only encouragement to call upon their own sensibilities. Rely on children's intuitive feelings and natural talent to ac-

3. For anthologies of black and Afro-Antillean poets, see Bibliography.

complish what they set out to do. (For details, see "Children Make Music," p. 188.) The end product will undoubtedly satisfy their peers. Contributing in his own way allows every child the chance to enjoy a feeling of personal success, essential to continuing growth. Even the accompanist must decode the words in order to convey the spirit of the piece in the accompaniment.

Three short poems by Langston Hughes will serve to show how a sensitive selection of instruments can support meaning. Each of these poems calls for a different style of accompaniment. The poetic idea is expressed with words that *sound* bright, sharp, or splendid. Their quality can be captured with instruments and rhythms that *sound* bright, sharp, or splendid. Thus free expressiveness follows as a result of thought and study.

Heaven [4]

Heaven is
The place where
Happiness is
Everywhere.

Animals
And Birds sing—
As does
Everything.

To each stone,
"How-do-you-do?"
Stone answers back,
"Well! And you?"

Motto [5]

I play it cool
And dig all jive.

4. *Selected Poems of Langston Hughes* (New York: Alfred A. Knopf, 1969).

5. *The Poetry of the Negro 1746–1970*, ed. Langston Hughes and Arna Bontemps (Garden City, N.Y.: Doubleday, 1970).

That's the reason
I stay alive.

My motto,
As I live and learn,
    is:
Dig and Be Dug
In Return.

My People [6]

The night is beautiful,
So the faces of my people.

The stars are beautiful,
So the eyes of my people.

Beautiful, also, is the sun.
Beautiful, also, are the souls of my people.

It is hard to choose or to stop at three poems; Langston Hughes has written so many of significance. For those studying American history, there are "October 16" (about John Brown at Harper's Ferry) and "Democracy"; "Dream Variations," "Water-Front Streets," and a host of others build pride in being black.

Follow-Ups

Hearing poetry or prose read aloud by teacher or classmates, and looking through anthologies to find an example of particular interest, often lead boys and girls far afield when they become deeply involved with subject matter.

6. *Selected Poems.*

Nellie, a twelve-year old, asked her teacher to read aloud a poem called "Jamaica Market" by Agnes Maxwell-Hall. Nellie had discovered the poem while browsing through *3000 Years of Black Poetry.*[7]

Honey, pepper, leaf-green limes,
Pagan fruit whose names are rhymes,
Mangoes, breadfruit, ginger-roots,
Granadillas, bamboo shoots,

Cho-cho, ackees, tangerines,
Lemons, purple Congo-beans,
Sugar, okras, kola-nuts,
Citrons, hairy coconuts,

Fish, tobacco, native hats,
Gold bananas, woven mats,
Plantains, wild-thyme, pallid leeks,
Pigeons with their scarlet beaks,

Oranges and saffron yams,
Baskets, ruby guava jams,
Turtles, goat-skins, cinnamon,
Allspice, conch shells, golden rum.

Black skins, babel—and the sun
That burns all colours into one.

Everyone in the class was enthusiastic about this poem. The teacher paused after every few lines in response to waving hands of children who wanted to describe one of the foods or articles not often come upon in the city. Those who had seen some of the foods growing tried to tell others how they grew and what they looked like.

The teacher's suggestion of visiting a local market was loudly acclaimed, and a project that lasted several weeks was initiated. Some of the foods mentioned in the poem were bought, examined in class and then those that could be eaten raw were

7. *3000 Years of Black Poetry*, ed. Alan Lomax and Raoul Abdul (New York: Dodd, Mead, 1970).

divided to give everyone a taste. Parents, grandparents, relatives, and friends became aware of the children's enthusiasm and either sent recipes to school or discussed with children how some of their favorite dishes were prepared so that they in turn could report to their classmates.

Marguerita brought a pamphlet to class titled *Typical Puerto Rican Food Dishes* [8] which attracted a lot of attention. Children pored over the pamphlet and found in it a couple of pages on the nutrient value of single portions of many of the foodstuffs they knew. The pamphlet also contained typical menus and mouth-watering recipes with specific directions for size of cans for numbers of consumers and directions for mixing and/or cooking.

One group of children, after reading practically every recipe in the book to find something to make for the class, finally settled on Pigeon Peas Salad. The recipe given was to serve 6 so in order to arrive at the number of cans of pigeon peas and onions to buy, a bit of division was necessary (6 into the number of people in the class). The oil and vinegar, in fractional quantities, were brought from home by individuals; then poured into a measuring container for everyone to observe a demonstration of addition of fractions.

Pigeon Peas Salad

(ENSALADA DE GANDULES)

(SERVES 6)

1 can cooked pigeon peas #2
¼ teaspoon pepper
½ cup oil
¼ cup vinegar
1 onion in slices

8. *Typical Puerto Rican Food Dishes* is available from the Commonwealth of Puerto Rico, Migration Division, Department of Labor, 322 West 45 Street, New York, N.Y. 10036.

1. Add salt to pigeon peas to taste, also pepper
2. Arrange pigeon peas in a platter
3. Combine oil and vinegar and add to pigeon peas
4. Cover with onion slices

The time reading the pamphlet was well spent considering the amount of deciphering the experience entailed. Although the pamphlet was printed in English, the Spanish titles of recipes and kinds of food they called for gave the Spanish-speaking children a chance to show their prowess. Everyone benefited from the experience.

One thing led to another. Children began talking about all kinds of food, some they liked, some they didn't. A few questions turned the conversation to other sensory impressions— smell and sight—and how both affect taste.

Children were on the alert for other reading material that mentioned food. Donald came upon the word *ackee*, a word unfamiliar to him until he had learned it from "Jamaica Market." He found it in a folk verse called "Linstead Market" [9] which presented a different point of view about buying and selling food.

> Carry me ackee, go to Linstead Market;
> Not a quarter would sell.
> Carry me ackee, go to Linstead Market;
> Not a quarter would sell.

> (REFRAIN) Oh, Lawd! not a mite not a bite,
> What a Saturday night!
> Oh, Lawd! not a mite, not a bite,
> What a Saturday night!

> Everybody come—fill up, fill up;
> Not a quarter would sell.

9. Beatrice Landeck, *Echoes of Africa* (New York: David McKay, 1961, 1969).

Ev'rybody come—fill up, fill up;
Not a quarter would sell.

(Repeat REFRAIN)

Make me call it louder, Ackee! Ackee!
Red and pretty they am.
Lady buy your Sunday morning breakfast,
Rice and ackee am gran'.

(Repeat REFRAIN)

This poem was in a form that could be arranged for different speakers with a refrain that everyone joined in on. Several children worked together before performing it for the class. They made their own rhythmic accompaniment by clapping hands and tapping feet in syncopated style.

But there was still more to come. Elinora discovered "The Tropics in New York" by Claude McKay: [10]

Bananas ripe and green, and ginger-root,
Cocoa in pods and alligator pears,
And tangerines and mangoes and grapefruit,
Fit for the highest prize at parish fairs.

Set in the window, bringing memories
Of fruit-trees laden by low-singing rills,
And dewy dawns, and mystical blue skies
In benediction over nun-like hills.

My eyes grew dim, and I could no more gaze;
A wave of longing through my body swept,
And, hungry for the old, familiar ways,
I turned aside and bowed my head and wept.

She read only the first verse but when the teacher helped out

10. Langston Hughes and Arna Bontemps, eds., *The Poetry of the Negro* (Garden City, N.Y.: Doubleday, 1970).

on the other verses, a new subject was brought up for discussion. Why were some foods so closely associated with a way of life? Could it be because they suggest a familiar environment associated with home? The class as a whole seemed to understand what this poem was about.

By Christmas time everyone was looking for something that might interest the class, each child seriously tackling the problem of decoding according to his own ability and freely calling on classmates and teacher for help when needed. Douglas, who had begun slowly, came upon a Frank Horne poem, "Kid Stuff," in which the words *wise guys* caught his attention. With help he managed to sound out familiar words and soon became involved in the meaning of the poem.

When he read it aloud in Word Lab his classmates saw possibilities for arranging the poem for choral speaking. This they did under Douglas's direction. Their arrangement rose to a dynamic climax at the beginning of the third verse and then gradually diminished to a quiet ending.

Kid Stuff [11]

SMALL GROUP: *The wise guys*
tell me
that Christmas
is Kid Stuff . . .

1ST SINGLE VOICE: *Maybe they've got*
something there—

THREE CHILDREN: *Two thousand years ago*
three wise guys
chased a star
across a continent

11. Ibid.

2ND SINGLE VOICE: *to bring*
                     frankincense and myrrh
                     to a Kid
                     born in a manger

3RD SINGLE VOICE: *with an idea in his head . . .*

WHOLE GROUP: *And as the bombs*
                     crash
                     all over the world
                     today

THREE CHILDREN: *the real wise guys*
                     know

WHOLE GROUP: *that we've all*
                     got to go chasing stars
                     again

SMALL GROUP: *in the hope*
                     that we can get back
                     some of that
                     Kid Stuff

4TH SINGLE VOICE: *born two thousand years ago—*

Reading Competitions

An extra incentive for making a personal selection can be given by arranging a competitive oral performance of literature children choose to work on. To do this, a class would organize a monthly contest and award a title to the student whose piece was chosen as the favorite for that month. Fancy titles add to to fun. Winner for the month might be called *Mighty Inspector* or *Grand Investigator of Literature*.

Such a contest would get children down to books and it would also promote reading aloud, for choosing a winning piece necessitates several rereadings for semifinals and finals. Adding a musical background to recitations of the winners of several months makes a fitting performance for an assembly program or for an early evening program for parents.

Children's Books

Scores of children's books pertaining to Afro-American and Afro-Antillean cultures are steadily being published. Several annotated bibliographies,[12] dealing explicitly and exclusively with these publications, can be consulted in the local branch of the Public Library.

The educational division of every major publishing house has a Black History and/or Black Culture series; some of them list titles pertaining to Afro-Antillean culture. Multi-media kits, filmstrips, transparencies, and other aids are also available.

In addition, several smaller publishing houses have specialized in Resources for Black Studies,[13] including some organized for the very purpose of servicing the needs of black- and Latin-American children of elementary school age. An example of this group is New Dimensions Publishing Company, headed by a black man, John Hines. Their 1974 catalogue includes five series of books: *Teaching Reading Skills through Drama*, *Africa Series*, *Puerto Rico Series* (bilingual), *Drug Prevention Series* (bilingual), and *Spanish*. Most of the readers are on a fourth- to fifth-grade reading level but contain subject material of interest to young people through ninth grade. Readers from the first series mentioned above are presented in dramatic form, each "lends itself to being mounted as dramas for class projects."

12. For annotated bibliographies of children's books focused on black and Latin cultures, see Bibliography in Appendix I.

13. For partial listing of minority-owned publishing houses specializing in black and Latin resources in children's books, see Bibliography in Appendix I.

Another possible source of books sure to interest a particular class would be books from a child's personal collection at home. Ask children to bring their favorite book to school to share with the class. Be sure the book is clearly marked as the property of the child so that it will be returned. Some children's books from the West Indies in English, Spanish, and French are not easy to obtain. Several obvious purposes are served by introducing them into the classroom.

Creative Writing as a Collective Experience

7

Johnny Gets the Word

It is one thing to learn the skill of writing, another to have something to *say* in writing. The impetus for *creative* writing comes from the desire to express ideas rather than to learn how to write. Since children stimulate each other's thought processes, collective composition has certain advantages over independent work.

This is not the time to work on spelling, sentence structure, or punctuation. Fear of being corrected impedes spontaneity and causes a child to lose interest in the project. When children apply themselves with seriousness of purpose, they learn from each experience. Progress may be slow, but as in all education, the will to learn is a first step in learning.

Free Verse

Short lines in verse form, contributed by children orally as an idea occurs to them, facilitates class composition. Once the ideas are spontaneously expressed, each child writes down his or her contribution so that it can be arranged by the class as a whole into a composition. Ideas abound if the given theme captures children's interest.

Sometimes children work in teams to help each other get the words on paper. Another time, a teacher might write the words on the board for a child to copy. Procedures depend on students' facility but always with the prevailing attitude that the recording of the idea is for the purpose of making it usable in a joint project.

Pop Poems

Pop poems are the literary equivalent of pop art, developed by poets as a kind of game. Pop or "found" poems are constructed by putting together in a design printed signs seen on city streets, directions for use of equipment, labels, or any other concise language in print that strikes the fancy. They have two tremendous advantages in working with children; no grammatical construction is involved, and they are built with words children know.

I once introduced pop poems to a class of second graders by reading a poem called "Yield," [1] which has to do with traffic signs. The children quickly caught the idea and claimed that they could write a poem as good as that. Realizing that the task involved reading as well as writing, I asked them to look for street signs on their way home and to be prepared the next day to write on the board the ones they chose for the poem.

1. Ronald Gross, *Pop Poems* (New York: Simon & Schuster, 1967).

The idea fascinated them. They could scarcely wait to write the words on the board as they arrived in the morning. Then, as one child pointed to the words of each sign in turn, the children who suggested it called it out together. Those who did not recognize all the words at first learned them by listening to other children. And, because there were duplications of simple signs like STOP and GO, the poorer readers were in their glory when their word came up.

Children copied from the board whatever words they chose to work with in their notebooks. They arranged them in an order they liked, to make their own short pop poem. I suggested that they might want to combine opposites to add to the fun. Child after child read his/her poem aloud and everyone had a chance to make suggestions for additions, deletions, substitutions, and order changes until they arrived at a composite version which I wrote on the board.

As the class read the poem aloud in unison, some boys started adding sound effects, such as screeching brakes after the word STOP. This suggested another idea: they gave their poem a rhythm of two beats to a line with a free unmeasured vocal sound effect after the last line of each stanza. By the time the poem was completed, everyone in the class recognized every word. This is how it shaped up, recited in two slow beats per line:

    TURN LEFT
       TURN RIGHT
         WALK
         WAIT   —(Sound of horn blowing
                               impatiently)
                           (Policeman's whistle)

   ONE WAY
      PARK HERE
        YIELD
         GO   —(Sound of car starting up)

```
SCHOOL CROSSING
   BLASTING                —(pow inserted without up-
                             setting rhythm)
        PARKING METER
        SQUEEZE            —(Eeee—ze—)


   NO DEPOSIT
   NO RETURN
   NO STANDING
   STOP                    —(Complete silence)
```

Children in a third-grade class were amused and inspired by the poem the second-graders had written and followed it up with poems made from all sorts of different printed material. Directions on boxtops (*push here, press down, pull out*) were combined in a verse that was hung in the hall, where it attracted the attention of children in other grades who then were eager to make poems of their own. Various forms were experimented with. One class gave their poem a percussion accompaniment as well as vocal sound effects. Another used cumulative form— added to every stanza the last lines of all the preceding stanzas in reverse order.

A sixth-grade class used this pop poem for choral speaking, assigning parts for solo and chorus. It served well as a vehicle for satisfying their love of making sounds per se, created within the bounds of an organized frame and dignified by the label *poem*.

Pop poems opened the children's eyes to printed matter of many kinds, and got them interested in the rhythm and sound of words and the written symbols that represent the sound. It was a project that helped both reading and writing because youngsters enjoyed finding the words as well as organizing them into a poem.

Wishes, Lies, and Dreams

A class project of a more aesthetic nature was initiated by the poet Kenneth Koch, whose work with children was described in his book *Wishes, Lies, and Dreams* published in 1970, followed by a second book in '73.[2] Koch started to teach poetry writing to children in a New York elementary school under the sponsorship of the Academy of American Poets, and then of the Teachers' and Writers' Collaborative. Included in his first book is an essay describing his approach.

He tells how he began by asking everyone in a fourth-grade class to write a single line beginning with the words "I wish." He told the children not to worry about spelling and to write after the first two words whatever they really wished for. The lines, unsigned, were read aloud in sequence. Koch writes about this first collaboration:

> The children were enormously excited by writing the lines and even more by hearing them read as a poem. They were talking, waving, blushing, laughing, and bouncing up and down.

Wishes were followed by Comparison poems, Noise poems, Dream poems, Color poems, Lie (not "make-believe") poems. Koch did not grade or evaluate the work done—he advised, he encouraged, and the children's poems were better with every try. New ideas were introduced in warm-up sessions: to get children away from clichés, he'd ask questions like, "What color is Los Angeles?" "What object in the classroom most resembles the overcast sky?" He taught them to think like poets, but he says, "Teaching really is not the right word for what takes place: it is more like permitting the children to discover something they already have."

2. Kenneth Koch, *Wishes, Lies, and Dreams* (New York: Random House, 1970). Paperback. Kenneth Koch, *Rose, Where Did You Get That Red?* (New York: Random House, 1973).

In his work with children, he instilled a respect for language—all language, everyone's language. Some poems used mixed Spanish and English words, others were written entirely in Spanish. For some children, this was the first time they had been able to use and be proud of their own language in school.

Kenneth Koch's second book, *Rose, Where Did You Get That Red?*, is equally helpful to teachers and parents. In both books he maintains that children have a natural talent for writing poetry and that they love doing it. But they need an impetus for putting thoughts on paper and confidence in knowing that what they do is of value.

It is pertinent here to point out that Koch gave his students a frame for their writing. Although they had complete freedom in expressing their thoughts, they were given a subject and usually the first two words of their line. With this amount of direction, their minds were focused rather than bewildered by infinite possibilities.

Furthermore, they began by building a poem as a class so that everyone was involved in the project. The interaction of the children gave an added thrust to the original impetus.

Cultural Identity

Children's original writing is markedly affected by a teacher's attitudes and concepts which inevitably permeate a classroom environment. Curriculum materials also reflect a teacher's personal convictions. For example, due to pressures exerted by the profession, changes were made in the illustrations of textbooks that pictured Mother habitually wearing an apron, hovering near the kitchen, and Father going off to work or playing ball with the boys. This kind of male and female stereotyping is no longer tolerated.

But a similar indoctrination takes place in culturally pluralistic classes when children are exposed exclusively to materials of Euro-American culture. Middle-class white children are subtly but forcefully impressed by the superiority of white culture. Children of ethnic groups make equally false judgments in deeming their own culture inferior.

A recent book, oddly titled *The Forsaken Lover*,[3] presents a potent argument against the imposition of a foreign culture on young children. It brings out the futility of negation; the basic need of all children to express themselves naturally and to utilize their real life experience for creative writing.

"The Forsaken Lover" is the title of a poem written by a black child in an attempt to write white words. Chris Searle used the same title for his book—satirically to point out the inappropriateness of the student's composition. The subtitle is *White Words and Black People*. Searle makes an excellent case against the exclusive use of English literature in teaching black Trinidadian children. He maintains that black children are not only robbed of their identity by being immersed in a literature foreign to their culture but further that they learn to condemn themselves when they imitate in their own writing the literature of whites. In Searle's opinion, white literature, however subtly, vindicates and praises whiteness; he cites many examples of English classics to prove his point.

In addition, Searle gives various examples of children's original work which is free of "foreign" indoctrination. An especially interesting one is on the subject of Carnival. In proper home language rather than in school language, the young writer paints a vivid picture of the excitement of 'Mas and describes incidents that made her forget to be home by the appointed hour of nine o'clock. Her work is honest and convincing. By writing of her own world in dialectal style, she produces a unique piece of writing. I know of no other in the English language that does as much justice to this yearly celebration.

The latter part of the book is devoted to a Drama of Identity, created and enacted by students. It deals with an

---

3. Chris Searle, *The Forsaken Lover: White Words and Black People* (London: Routledge & Kegan Paul, 1972).

island hurricane they had experienced. Built from short essays several thirteen-year-olds had written, describing what they saw and how they felt, the framework of the play was mapped out by Searle with guidelines for individual speeches to be improvised by the children. It has the ring of truth and genuineness that the poem "The Forsaken Lover" lacks so spectacularly.

Allowing children to write creatively on relevant themes and in their accustomed language is a vital part of their education. The purpose is to gain facility in verbal expression. Learning another mode of expression can only *follow* facility with words one knows.

When a child learns school English she/he will recognize the time and place proper for each style of communication, but never will the native tongue be discarded or forgotten. An educated person uses standard and nonstandard interchangeably as each is suitable to a given situation. As a single telling example of a man well known for his eloquence, Martin Luther King shouted to his fellow marchers when they reached their goal in Montgomery, Alabama, "We ain't gonna let nobody turn us around!" Quoting the nonstandard language of the spiritual served as a powerful statement under the circumstances!

A cogent analogy between school and home language was made by William Raspberry in an article that appeared in the April, 1970 issue of *Today's Education*. The following is a quote from the article:

> The reason we want slum children to learn standard is that non-standard is a good deal less negotiable—just as trading stamps are less negotiable than cash. But that doesn't mean that trading stamps are *bad*. It is here the linguists make the heart of their case. The way we speak is such an integral part of who we are that to deprecate our speech is to deprecate us.
>
> What the linguists want to do is to give slum children facility with their native non-standard—to give them cash

without confiscating their trading stamps. The non-standard, lest we forget, may be *the* negotiable language back home in the slum neighborhood or within the family or on the playground. After all, you can't pay cash for that lamp at the redemption center.

If substantial numbers of teachers believe non-standard equals stupid, then forget linguistics. Forget everything, for any teacher so insensitive that he will shame a child into silence every time he opens his mouth is beyond the help even of the Center for Applied Linguistics.

Language Events

If a teacher is looking for a way really to involve upper-grade children of ethnic background in creative writing, a sure-fire strategy is to have them prepare for a Language Event, a traditional part of Afro-Antillean festivities. This is a verbal contest in which contestants come from the masses, from those untutored young people in hamlet or town who have a natural flair with words. If children know the custom—as many of them do—they know that these language events call for *people's* language which actually *encourages* them to use their native tongue in school. However paradoxical this may seem, we shall see that using their own manner of speech, black or Spanish, leads to a knowledge and use of school English.

In Puerto Rico, the Language Event is part of Christmas celebrations. It comes off as a competition between two bards who are given a subject for an on-the-spot improvisation. While one performs, the other thinks up his verse—traditionally a ten-line stanza with eight beats to a line known as a *décima*. Although the subject for improvisation is unknown in advance, the form allows for repetition, nonsense syllables, and stock phrases that are on the tip of every bard's tongue. The musical background is essentially rhythmical, primarily a frame for the words.

On islands of English-speaking people, contests are also held annually, but usually before Carnival, to audition young amateurs who have prepared lyrics *in advance* on a calypso rhythm (which also has eight beats to the line). Performers accompany themselves on a guitar backed by a band for the occasion. The winner is named Calypso King of the year.

Décimas

Children of Puerto Rican parents are apt to know about *décimas* because many families who live on the mainland carry on the homeland tradition at Christmas parties. At such a time, they adapt the traditional form: two members of the party alternately make up one *line* (instead of a verse) to compete with each other. They brag, tease, joke, and challenge one another to greater efforts. In this informal setting, the *décima* has no set number of lines; it continues until one of the two gives up.

When ideas are slow in forthcoming—at community celebrations or at home—a contestant fills the line with vocal syllables such as *lei-lo-lei* (repeated), or with singing syllables *do-re-mi*, or with letters of the alphabet, *hachi-i-jota-ka*. Imitating this practice in class, children can familiarize themselves with the *seis* rhythm as those who know it render it in percussion. If they want an assist from a recording, the instrumental record played for dancing the *bomba* (p. 88) will help out.

To help children further in becoming comfortable with the style of the frame they will work with, volunteers might demonstrate how one after another line is spoken in a mock battle of words. Spanish-speaking children raise hands when they are ready and speak their line as the teacher acknowledges them. They may repeat lines they have heard, make up one on the spot, or fill the line with nonsense syllables.

If they then translate a few lines into English or even give the jist of them, the English-speaking boys and girls will get in the spirit of the contest and possibly be ready to try a similar alternation of voices.

Let the class choose a subject they can handle—like *Why I come to school*—which allows for opposing positions and different points of view. After children agree on an opening line, each child writes his response to that line, purposely refuting it or giving a teasing response.

Children who want to read their line aloud will undoubtedly inspire others to get into the play. Making up a *décima* attracts boys and girls because of the opportunity to kid a supposed opponent. If you see that the English-speaking children respond enthusiastically, suggest that they develop a *décima* in teams to perform for members of the class or for a larger assembly as will be described for calypso contests (p. 155).

In any case, the experience will stand them in good stead when the similar custom of English-speaking people in the Caribbean is introduced. All children know calypso lyrics because they have been popular in the United States. The two verbal contests can be worked on simultaneously with children making the choice of which form they prefer to present in a Language Event.

Antillean Calypso

Like *décimas*, subjects for *calypso* performances cover a wide range of topics but whether they be serious or comic, the originator of a calypso lyric communicates his observations in a down-to-earth manner with an ingenuousness that sets it apart from other folklore. No figurative meaning is implied but familiar words are presented in unconventional garb. An uncommon expression describes a common occurrence in defiance of a rigid use of language.

Children are drawn to colorful language and unorthodox phraseology. They enjoy talking about different ways to say something and in the discussion, comparing the deviant to proper school English. In this context of pure enjoyment, what they learn sticks by them.

A familiar lyric such as "Water Come-A Me Eye" brings the subject in focus. The meaning is obvious but the unique way of expressing it evokes a vivid picture in few words.

1. Ev'ry time I 'memba Liza,
Water come-a me eye.
Ev'ry time I think of Liza,
Water come-a me eye.

REFRAIN: *Come back, Liza, come back gal,*
Water come-a me eye.
Come back, Liza, come back gal,
Water come-a me eye.

2. I'm still waitin' home for Liza,
Water come-a me eye.
Heart is sore but waiting, Liza,
Water come-a me eye.

REFRAIN: *Come back, Liza, come back gal,*
Water come-a me eye.
Come back, Liza, come back gal,
Water come-a me eye.

Children recognize that *Water come-a me eye* describes a feeling. Perhaps they can describe the same feeling with other words writing one line, in the same number of beats. The following illustrates:

"Tears rise up in me eye"
"Water run down on me cheek"

Other physical reactions occur from feelings, such as:

"Heart go-a bump-a-ty bump"
"Knees go-a wishy-a-wash"

After several possibilities are explored, draw children's attention to personalizing the verse to go with the refrain they choose. "What makes tears come to your eyes or makes your heart beat loud or your knees shake?" A few suggestions bring forth genuine responses from children. For example, you could ask, "Did you cry when your best friend moved away from the neighborhood—when you moved away from a place you lived a long time?" Some children will write a verse on this topic, substituting the name of the person or place they miss for *Liza* in the original and following it with the refrain that describes their emotion. Thus a four-lined verse and a four-line refrain are composed by thinking up only one line for each. A truly rewarding undertaking!

Similarly, the mention of an anticipated treat will start children thinking about the excitement that causes the heart to *go-a bump-a-ty bump.* Someone in the class is sure to point out that running too fast does the same thing. Let each one who has something to say write it down following the model of the verse and refrain.

The idea of *knees go-a wishy-a-wash* concerns fear, an emotion often experienced by children. The privacy that the written word affords might encourage some children to reveal more than they would be willing to voice before a class.

From this simple beginning children learn to express in writing thoughts and concerns on a variety of subjects. Once in the habit of writing down what they want to write down within a given frame, they will be eager to extend their writing into larger forms. But to motivate all the children in a class for collective composition, a dance form they like and respond to gets things off to a good start.

Children who have lived in the West Indies know many calypso songs; those who have not undoubtedly have heard some which have reached these shores as pop hits. A wall chart of "Jamaica Farewell," for example, or of "Hill and Gully Rider," of "Rookumbine," "Better Take Warning," "Stop the Carnival," or other popular calypso songs is bound to attract the attention of boys and girls who are familiar with the words. Any of these lyrics or others they suggest can be used for language study in Word Lab. If it seems worthwhile to pursue the writing further, introduce the idea of preparing for a Language Event to be held for an audience other than the class.

Classroom Preparation

The idea of holding a language contest impels students to play with ideas for subjects and to experiment further in periods supplementary to the Word Lab. Heads will become buried in notebooks, and the notebooks will be exchanged. A few children may prefer to work alone, but most children want to join others for a team project.

Inevitably a group will want to try out lines in Word Lab. Suggestions for repetition of words and short phrases or repetitions with slight changes come from the other children. When a stanza is rounded out, everyone listens, tapping feet or snapping fingers on the beat and making vocal noises to mark the offbeats; the verse is shaped into syncopated calypso style. Lines written by other groups are heard and shaped in a similar way. A chorus part evolves in the process.

The poems or verses children write are almost always in a humorous vein and, like the model, phrased in unconventional language. A couplet of a few words airs a bit of classroom gossip, describes or teases an unnamed show-off, lampoons a school authority or political figure. But it is all in good fun. An audition committee composed of a boy or girl from each team rules on what topics can properly be included, and discusses the complete presentation of the verses.

Most contestants want a background of an instrumental group. If the instruments (a tin whistle, popular in the West Indies and Africa and easy to play, and a guitar and drum) are available, children are capable of creating a tune and "riff" and of independently organizing and rehearsing an instrumental group for performance. If they have a tape recorder to use, they gain considerably by hearing their rehearsals played back.

Some of the instrumentalists may want to work out a dance routine with a physical interpretation of the idea. If the thought occurs to them, they can design the "choreography" and plan with the soloist the staging of the performance.

Letting children plan and rehearse a program according to their own lights with supportive help from a teacher results in a production properly gauged to their level of sophistication. Such an approach promotes children's sense of responsibility, and discipline problems become minimal for no child dares to spoil the event for his peers. Each child's involvement in the project cancels out the disruptive behavior that is normally caused by lack of participation.

In the final performance, including *décimas* in Spanish or English interspaced with calypso will add spice to the program because of the difference between the two forms. Also, the event takes on importance if the final competition can be held in an assembly of several classes with an invited audience. The volume of applause determines the winners.

Thus through a challenging, enjoyable experience children gain some facility with words—their own words—and gain the courage to express ideas. At the same time, they become aware of differences in languages and different ways to communicate the same idea. In the course of the project a teacher has many opportunities to call attention to words and sentences in standard English and children have many opportunities to use school English in relation to the project.

Parables as a Springboard

Most of the material discussed so far has appealed to children's love of fun. However, to make the most of ethnic folklore in promoting creative writing, a teacher needs to help students to think conceptually, to probe for deeper meaning than a literal interpretation of words supply. As pointed out in earlier chapters, the poetry of spirituals in particular is rich in metaphor. The well-known ones abound in poetic symbolism; they convey an abstract concept made understandable through concrete representation (see p. 54).

Action lyrics are plentiful. "Hold On" has a plow as its symbol; many have means of locomotion such as trains or "wings to fly"; Jacob has a ladder to climb; a chariot (cart to carry cotton) is "comin' for to carry me home." Talking about the symbolism not only gets boys and girls thinking about vital subjects but also motivates them to express their own thoughts in writing.

A parable is an extended use of metaphor. Studying parables, based on Bible stories, can inspire creative writing. Many children are familiar with stories about Noah, David and Goliath, Moses, and numerous others. Discussion of these stories may suggest a similar treatment of a contemporary subject.

A well-known lyric of great substance can serve as a springboard for a writing project. Phrased in the vernacular, "Hosanna" is a work chant from Jamaica. The subject is based on the parable of the wise man who built his house on rock ("it fell not when the floods came"), and the foolish man who built on sand ("and great was the fall of his house"). The following version is from *Echoes of Africa in Folksongs of the Americas*.[4]

LEADER	RESPONSE
Hosanna!	
Me build me house, O!	*Ha, Ha!*
Me build 'pon sandy ground!	*Ha, Ha!*
The rain come wet it up;	*Ha, Ha!*
The sun come burn it up;	*Ha, Ha!*
The river wash it 'way;	*Ha, Ha!*
The storm come blow it down!	*Ha, Ha!*
The house is weak you see;	*Ha, Ha!*
The house done gone you see!	*Ha, Ha!*

4. Beatrice Landeck, *Echoes of Africa in Folksongs of the Americas* (New York: David McKay, 1961, 1969).

Hosanna!
Me build me house, O!   *Ha, Ha!*
Me build 'pon rocky ground!   *Ha, Ha!*
The rain come fall 'pon it;   *Ha, Ha!*
The sun come shine 'pon it;   *Ha, Ha!*
The house is strong you see!   *Ha, Ha!*
Me build 'pon rocky ground!   *Hosanna!*
Me build me house, O!   *Ha, Ha!*
Me build 'pon rocky ground!

The lyrics of "Hosanna" can launch a discussion of the imagery in parables, of the ethical implications of this parable for children's lives, and of other concepts that can be expressed in a parable. The metaphor of building houses for the building of character on strong or shaky ground is a striking image quickly perceived by young minds.

Having analyzed the concept of this parable, let the class decide what general idea they wish to convey and what accustomed action or familiar object could best symbolize their idea. Children choose subjects that reflect their immediate interests or concerns and treat them according to their understanding and level of maturity.

For example, a fifth-grade class worked out a composition on the theme, "*If you don't work, you don't eat.*" Using words of both black and white speech, they described the actions of a *hummer* who found many diversions from chores and as a result, did not have money to buy anything on the way home from school. Another boy, a *heavy*, earned enough money through minor *gigs* to buy himself two hot dogs.

A sixth-grade class worked on a different level. They chose the symbol of a trumpet to convey the character of human behavior. This was a subject that fired the imagination of every boy and girl in the class. Each had a contribution to make, and each tried to outdo the other purposely using expressions in the vernacular.

They planned their arrangement in Word Lab, deciding on

three verses of eight lines, each stanza to be introduced with
Now Listen and each line to be followed by *Wha-hah!*, closely
resembling the form of "Hosanna." The first verse was to be
happy, in the second something was to go wrong, and punish-
ment followed in the third verse. Children formed three groups
to work in supplementary periods with an adult in each. After
a great deal of interaction between groups in Lab time, which
involved class auditions and innumerable changes, the following poem evolved:

LEADERS FOR SINGLE LINES	RESPONSE
Now Listen!	
That horn blows cool—O!	*Wha-hah!*
That horn she shine so bright	*Wha-hah!*
She sound so groovy sweet	*Wha-hah!*
She sound so loud and hot	*Wha-hah!*
That horn she blow me mind	*Wha-hah!*
You see she make me light!	*Wha-hah!*
Sometime she play a moan	*Wha-hah!*
Sometime she play a groan.	*Wha-hah!*
Now Listen!	
That horn did burn—O!	*Wha-hah!*
The preacher say *Not here!*	*Wha-hah!*
Me try to make it sweet	*Wha-hah!*
Horn sounds a sour note	*Wha-hah!*
Me ma she yank me home	*Wha-hah!*
A cuff on ear, po' ear!	*Wha-hah!*
Me pa wait till I come	*Wha-hah!*
Me pa was mad, you see!	*Wha-hah!*
Now Listen!	
Pa blow me horn—O!	*Wha-hah!*
That trumpet moan a groan	*Wha-hah!*
Pa take me horn in hand	*Wha-hah!*
He bust it all to smash	*Wha-hah!*
That horn go through some change!	*Wha-hah!*

Po' trumpet groan a moan   *Wha-hah!*
That horn done broke, you see!   *Wha-hah!*
That horn done gone, you see!   *Wha-hah!*

Talking Blues

Another manifestation of poetic expression that can be an inspiration and model for framing children's original ideas is the popular form of talking blues. Indigenous to the United States, the blues were generated in a heartfelt cry against the hardships blacks experienced as slaves. The original blues form began with a brief comment followed by a pause for breath and reflection. The phrase and pause were repeated, and a final line brought the lamentation to a close. The style has endured through years of development and permutation—it is the backbone of jazz and soul music, and has never lost its appeal.

Children in all grades enjoy hearing blues, and can make up a lyric for their own blues. The rhythm and shape of the blues present no problem to young people because they are familiar with the general pattern. They can also independently improvise an instrumental background with percussion, guitar, thumb piano, and available melody instruments. If a guitarist or pianist wants help on the harmonic structure of the blues, he can find simple patterns to follow in a music textbook.[5]

A sixth-grade class in a school in Delaware spent part of the last month of school experimenting with different forms and styles of delivery in preparation for graduation exercises. The number on the program that brought the house down was a talking blues, performed by one boy at a mike, supported by a guitarist strumming chords, two boys on drums, and a

5. Harmonic pattern for blues is detailed in *Basal Music Textbooks*, Grade 5 or 6.

chorus of voices. The soloist spoke in a syncopated rhythm with pauses for breath that were filled by the remarks of classmates:

SOLOIST	CHORUS
1. Now listen man! There's somethin' I'm gonna tell.	Yeah! yeah! Tell it, man, tell it! come on
Oh yeah, there's somethin' good I gotta tell And it won't take long Cause soon there'll be a bell.	Well man, tell it! No-o-o? We'll be waitin' for that bell.
2. Just eyeball these cats A-sittin' straight up here!	We see them cats, oh sure man we do!
Look close these cats A-sittin' straight up here!	We said we see them cats a-sitting straight up there.
They're dressed in their best 'Cause they know grad'ation's near.	Yeah, man they're sure enough dressed up fine.
3. We worked real hard, real hard, No play at all. I said we worked hard, real hard No play at all.	Did we hear ya right, man? No ball at all? You must be kiddin'.
We sure didn't make it here By playing ball.	Nooo-man, Noooo.
4. Slick chicks here latch on fine 'Deed, they're the ones Real hip, in the groove Yeah man, they're the ones Boot it to aces, baby, Nix out none!	(Drawn-out whistle) Ah! Yeah man! Tell it, man, tell it!

Children were motivated in their work by their natural enjoyment in doing something well. The subject matter drew on their interest in the contemporary style and, because it was already familiar material, it allowed them to express themselves in a creative way. Since Word Lab is a time for a whole class to work together, the simplest way to motivate children of different abilities in creative activity—and, at the same time, maintain the decorum appropriate to school—is to afford them a definite beginning and end of an activity.

Independent Writing

As has been pointed out, when children learn to read and write in a short form, they are well on the way to using what they know in other ways. And this they must do, for other subjects in the curriculum do not supply a framework for their writing nor do instructors in general look favorably on poetic answers when factual answers are called for.

There is no sharp cutoff, however, between creative writing as a collective experience and creative writing as an independent activity. The main difference between them is that in the collective experience, the whole class shares in the *act* of composition; while in independent writing, members of the class work by themselves to exchange their work later with others and together enjoy the fruits of individual composition. Collective composition and independent writing each has its place in the school day.

Recording Observations

To promote independent writing, a few minutes at the end of the day can be set aside for each child to jot down, in his/ her own diary (notebook), a sentence or two about the day at school. These would be personal and private notes written for a child's own satisfaction. They could be about anything that seemed important to the individual child, either in expressing his feelings or in recording an observation or event or even in writing a line or two of a riddle or joke in order to remember it.

Children should be encouraged to write without fear of being graded on what they say. Some children may use their writing (or picture-making) to let off steam. Others will be more anecdotal in their approach. At the elementary level, writing is more apt to be objective than introspective.

The sharing of written work happens gradually. One child asks another or the teacher for help in recalling an incident or in spelling a word and, little by little, as children take pride in what they do, diaries come to be freely exchanged and worked on together.

Class History

Using the recording of observations as a beginning, a collective history of the class can be written—a history of its development over the period of a school term. Some children will range wider than others, but if the anecdotal parts of the diaries are shared, girls and boys in upper grades will start borrowing techniques from each other, learning from each other, and leading each other to an objective evaluation of their school life.

However far they go, the initial fun of writing only for themselves, anything they want to write, and sharing only what they want to share, will develop their skill to a greater degree than if they are told what to write. For they will discover that writing itself is a deeply satisfying activity.

Exploring the Environment

In the fifth and sixth grades, students look beyond themselves and the classroom to explore family background and community. The magnitude of exploring the environment has been dealt with in a publication that can hardly be summarized here but is inexpensive enough for every classroom to own. It is called *Your City Has Been Kidnapped*.[6] On the inside of the paper cover, the following is inscribed:

> This book is about the mystery and magic that is city life. Depending on your interests, it can serve as a textbook, sensory guide, a source book for locating city treasure, an investigation manual into city institutions, or perhaps, a simple game book, for a rainy day.

This oversize book is made up of wall placards proposing ways for children in the San Francisco Bay Area to investigate their city environment. But the cogent, readable text is a guide that makes it applicable for any city dweller. Valuable for teachers as well as students, a number of pertinent questions on each page directs the reader's attention to looking, seeing, perceiving, comprehending, and understanding—thus enhancing every phase of day-by-day existence. Sharing reports of personal discoveries with others not only intensifies the individual's enjoyment but also stimulates others in the class to venture forth on their own.

Choice of Assignments

Provocative assignments might be posted on the bulletin board to encourage girls and boys to write reports or at the least take notes on exploring their neighborhood. There should be a sufficient number to appeal to different tastes so that children could honestly choose one that was of special interest. Among others, interviewing a grown-up you know should

6. W. Ron Jones, *Your City Has Been Kidnapped*, a Deschool Primer (San Francisco: Zephryus, 1972). Zephryus is a nonprofit collaborative of San Francisco Bay Area teachers, parents, toymakers, and friends. Write to: Zephryus Educational Exchange, 1201 Stanyan Street, San Francisco, Calif. 94117.

elicit some response that would furnish an interesting subject for class discussion in Word Lab. Give children who choose this assignment, a little direction by focusing the interview with suggestions for a few opening questions:

What were you doing when you were my age?

Were did you live?

Did you have brothers or sisters?

Who was the oldest?

What did you plan to do when you grew up?

Did you play games?

Go to school?

What did you do on holidays?

Did you dance, play instruments, know any songs?

Show me!

Personal History

In time, reports may touch on general historical questions which indicates that children want better to understand their personal history. And then, autobiographical inquiries merge into areas of common interest. At this point, a group of children who are ready can begin to use reference material in the study of the history they share.[7]

With elementary school children the development will be slow, but black and Latin children sooner or later will take interest in the study of their racial heritage, their ancestry, the political and social causes of their condition at different periods in history.

Children's oral reports to other members of the class awaken the interest of everyone who has made an effort to seek his roots. If the reporting group is encouraged to select

7. For historical reference materials, see Bibliography: Children's Books.

slides and filmstrips to illustrate their talk, no child will be untouched by data pertaining to their origins.[8] But, history begins at home. Children themselves must find what they need to piece together the picture of who they are.

Learning Through Creative Experiences

The evidence is overwhelming that when children are presented with material alien to their experience and are expected to absorb it, they are slow, diffident, insecure, and their performance is mediocre. But when the materials they work with come from themselves and their own environment, they are confident enough to take their education beyond passivity into enthusiastic activity and creativity.

If we accept the responsibility of educating children of minority cultures, is it not fair that we allot a reasonable portion of curriculum time to give them the opportunity to learn effectively in a way compatible with their culture?

No child of Euro-American culture will be penalized by the inclusion of Latin-American and black-American resources in the curriculum. On the contrary, the products of these resources have become so vital a part of the total environment that children can only benefit from a close view of vigorous cultures so widely disseminated. Furthermore, the collective activities that inevitably result from classwork with these resources offer children of any culture a creative way of learning.

Creative activities range from supplying words in a rhythmic framework to a perceptive view of self and environment, awakening minds and senses. Such activities should continue throughout the grades, gauged to individual abilities, with constant addition of significant materials to challenge deeper thinking and more enthusiastic responsiveness. As children gain greater freedom to express themselves, they recognize greater need for skills to communicate to fellow students and adults what they confidently feel is worthy of attention.

8. For audiovisual aids, see Bibliography: Children's Books.

Ethnic Music Related to Language Development

Reading By Ear

When children really enjoy musical experiences in a classroom, the walls between school and life outside come tumbling down. An affinity to music causes children to relax tensions, to forget conflicts, to be open and receptive to learning. Adults and children are drawn together, on a par, sharing an experience in which the children feel on sure ground.

Listening to music has positive values other than those derived from a study of the art. The importance of these experiences cannot be overestimated, especially for children of the poor. Since music of ethnic groups has not been thoroughly explored as an adjunct to language development, considerable space will be given it here with suggestions for materials and procedures helpful to classroom teachers.

Introducing music in Word Lab therefore is not for the purpose of teaching music. Rather is it to motivate children to work with words through a medium they love and understand. Youngsters find a source of strength in music; talking about listening experiences promotes valid growth in language expression. This is a step in a direct line with our main target of learning to read and write.

Ethnic Musical Experiences

Before children of minority cultures get to school they have heard a powerful amount of music—music on radio, TV, and records; music in churches, stores, and supermarkets; tambourine gospel; music at family and community gatherings, at performances of street theaters, street concerts, and jazzmobiles. They have heard singers and instrumentalists of top rank, have sung their songs, danced to their music, hummed and whistled tunes they remembered, beat out rhythmic patterns on anything and everything within reach. They are experienced and sophisticated in their own genre of music, which represents an organic part of their culture.

"Sheets of sound are what engulf the citizen of the American black community perhaps every day of his life. He is not necessarily born with music in his soul but he is definitely born to music in his environment," wrote Carman Moore in a feature article in the *New York Times*. "Therefore the black man often finds himself walking in a music-affirming gait, talking and gesturing in quasi-musical phrasing, and filling much of his conversation with discussions of music and musicians."

Children are constantly exposed to "sheets of sound" in their communities. Hearing music with a familiar sound in a different environment sets up a sympathetic vibration in them.

They become invigorated, voluble, confident. The world of music is their territory and, in the classroom, it provides fertile ground for cultivating their ability to express themselves in words.

The accumulating resources upon which ethnic performances draw today—from past and present—are vast, including many media and styles of expression: popular (soul, rhythm-and-blues, dance forms), folk and gospel, jazz as a popular and an art form, and concert music. Each of the categories (excepting gospel) with the designation of Latin before the title describes the Hispano-American style as well. Selections of music in all these categories have elements in common that children of every culture intuitively recognize and respond to. These, then, are the styles of music for experiences that can forward language development.

Popular Music

Because all schoolchildren hear popular music more often than any other type, they recognize the voice or instrumental sound of current performers. A good start in Word Lab is to play a recording of soul music, rhythm-and-blues, gospel, or Latin jazz. What a surprise for children to enter a classroom and hear the voice of a favorite vocalist or a solo by a famous instrumentalist accompanied by a Latin or black band. How much more this would say about what the day holds than any words a teacher could command!

Beginning a day this way takes little time as children are assembling and sets a tone for easy relationships among everyone. Only one selection should be played—it is better to repeat that than to introduce another—with title and name of performer written on the board.

Let children respond as they choose, imitating the style of the singer in their voices, beating out a rhythmic accompaniment, moving about the room. Young children as well as older should be allowed to react freely so long as their activity is related to the music and governed by its beginning and ending. Sometimes two or more children will devise a hand-clapping game, dance in a small circle or invent a pattern of movement. Other times, larger groups may take turns to perform calling for several repetitions of the music played.

Few children can ignore the stimulus of popular music at any age, even if they take part only by tapping feet and snapping fingers. Their respect for the beginning and ending of a piece imposes a limitation on the free activity and since a selection does not last more than two and a half minutes, the musical activity is of short duration even when a piece is repeated.

As the custom of listening is established, children want to choose the music themselves, bringing into the classroom selections from home or the library. After a child plays his choice, let him tell what he finds attractive about it. Others in the class will enter the discussion talking about the style of performance, the instrumentation, and especially the lyric. Is the selection on the charts or has it been around a long time? What type of song is it—soul, gospel, rhythm-and-blues, folk, protest? Does it have a rock accompaniment? What is the message of the lyric? Children readily speak out about a subject they know so well.

Skill Reinforcement

Lyrics of popular music introduce sophisticated words and ideas in Word Lab. But neither the words nor the topics are over the heads of children who have chosen them to play. Because the lyrics are related to children's thoughts and concerns, they can be used to reinforce techniques of writing in a self-directed activity. Ask three or four volunteers to write the title of a current hit they like on the board as suggestions for others to work on. A team of children may work together to write from memory verses of the song they choose from titles on the board. They help each other, prompting the recall of exact wording, correcting spelling, deciding on length of poetic lines, on order of verses. The team working on one lyric exchanges it with a team working on another until all are agreed on final versions. Then a spokesman for each team recites or sings a final copy for class approval.

Children in bilingual classes take part together in such an activity. The lyric that Spanish-speaking children know can be paraphrased by them, its general meaning translated so that everyone in the class understands. Similarly, English lyrics can be capsulized to highlight their essential meaning for Spanish-speaking classmates.

Children carry out this project mainly by themselves, with teachers or aides coming to their assistance when called upon. They supply the material for their own exercises and work cooperatively with classmates, using skills of reading and writing in a functional way.

Motivation for Study

There have been many articles reporting how ethnic music bolsters interest in school work especially for children of minority cultures. One of the most cogent articles dealing with this subject was titled "The Curriculum Is the Self." Written by Harry Morgan, dean of the Center for Afro-American Studies, Ohio University, Athens, it appeared in the December 1970 issue of the *Music Educators Journal*.

One section in the article recounts how a group of underachievers in the Ocean Hill–Brownsville section of Brooklyn participated in an afterschool music and dance project which was thought up by the children and Ronnie Simmons, a young paraprofessional fourth-grade teacher. Some brief excerpts concerning this project follow:

During the first afternoon they moved and reacted rhythmically to the music of popular soul records—building a relationship of substance through the music of their out-of-school life.

Group talk sessions evolved and led to discussions about the African and Caribbean rhythmic roots of soul music and about fundamental ethnic relationships between music of the old world and music of the third world.

The children were beginning to sense an identity they could be proud of—an identity that shattered the Hollywood version of their ancestors . . .

After conversation and discussions that arose from challenging and provocative questions, this highly successful project resulted in children creating a music-and-dance drama, inspired by the recording *Drums of Passion* by Baba Olatunji.[1] In planning it, they needed to research beyond what the teacher provided; for example they read the notes on the back of the record's jacket:

> Because they were highly motivated, the children were able to accomplish this normally difficult task. They interpreted the intricate phrasing and sentence structure for each other. The group went on to build a vocabulary, read, discuss, and share their new skills with other teachers who were beginning to see positive changes in them.

Why should all the fun and mind-expanding activities happen *after* school hours when they can properly take place in the classroom? Popular music meaningful to children motivates them to seek knowledge beyond what they already know. Not only jacket covers of recordings will be read but trade magazines about popular music, lying on open shelves, are also apt to attract the attention of children in the upper grades. One in particular gives considerable space to Latin "soul" as well as to black artists of rhythm-and-blues and gospel. It is

1. Baba Olatunji, *Drums of Passion* (Columbia CS-8210).

a weekly called *Record World*[2] and covers the high spots of record popularity across the country. It also carries a weekly column in Spanish, *"Nuestro Rincón,"* with an English translation. Such a magazine might well become a "reader" for middle- and upper-grade children.

Explicit Language Usage

A major factor in developing children's use of language is to encourage them to be more precise in their expressions. This may mean enlarging vocabulary but it also means using words that children already know.

Girls and boys can be helped to describe the genuine reactions they feel with unhackneyed words. The old clichés of feeling *sad, happy, scared* scarcely apply either to the current style of music or to the current style of children's reactions. Expecting students to identify their emotional involvement by naming stock emotions underestimates both the capacity and the intensity of their feelings.

Words boys and girls normally use among themselves are starters but a teacher can help them express themselves by suggesting that they compare their reactions to something they experience in daily living. For example, they might compare tempo to how fast or slow they move themselves; volume to noise in the environment; mood to some usual occurrence that engenders a similar mood.

In searching for analogies and explicit language, children's listening becomes focused on certain basic elements in music that can be named with words. Directing their attention to these elements through a kind of word game (rather than through theoretical study) gives listeners a substantial base for further enjoyment of any kind of music.

A few sample questions follow as suggestions for some

2. Record World, 1700 Broadway, New York, N.Y. 10019.

down-to-earth analogies. These would be used sparingly as an incidental part of class discussion if any one of them was pertinent to a particular piece of music. The idea is to encourage children to think of their own analogies in order to promote language usage, not to teach music.

Tempo

What is the beat of the music?

Is it fast? how fast? fast as you can jump or fast as a speed-car?

Is it slow, well how slow? like a shuffle?

What else moves as slowly as the beat of the music?

Questions that call for precise thinking call forth precise and sometimes colorful language. Fast and slow (tempo) are meaningless terms unless defined by a *rate* of movement. In comparing the movement of a piece to something everybody knows, *tempo* becomes a fascinating focus for listening.

Rhythmic Character

Closely related to tempo as an element in all music is *rhythmic character.*

Does the music you heard have sudden thrusts that throw you off-balance? (Syncopation)

Or is it smooth flowing like molasses?

Does it jump like popcorn popping in a popcorn machine?

Or is it solemn like a faucet dripping?

Does it hop along nervously like a pigeon picking up crumbs on a city street or does it rush into startled flight?

Is it steady like a count-down or a bouncing ball or
does it change speed like a bus on a crowded street,
slowing down for a light or speeding up to jump a
light?

Dynamics

Dynamics, another basic element in composition, is readily
recognized by children albeit not by that name. They know it
best through electronic instruments: if you turn the volume
up, it's loud; turn it down, it's soft. But there are degrees of
loud and soft.

How loud, how soft?

Loud as an explosion or rumbling like thunder?

Loud enough to make you cover your ears or soft as a
mumble or a whisper?

Does the volume change during the piece like people
arguing who raise their voice then quiet down?

Does the piece end with a smash or fade off into silence?

Mood

A fourth element common to every style and media of
music is *mood,* quickly perceived by children. In their own
language they might say, "Oooh, that bad!" (meaning *good*).
Or they might use the words *heavy, tough,* or *strong* to imply
a favorable reaction. Suggest that they go beyond a single ad-
jective to describe how the music makes them feel.

Is it lonely as left out?

Shiny as an *A*?

Weird like out-of-space?

Does it make your heart pound as if you ran too far and too fast?

Does it make you want to cry?

Is it far-out, freakish, crazy, or just plain sugar sweet?

A few suggestions strategically injected into conversation gives children the idea of making up their own descriptive phrases. They are apt to listen attentively to a particular element of the music in order to come up with something original that will make their peers laugh or applaud.

Using Notebooks

As children listen to music they may first want to experience it with some kind of movement. But on a repeat, suggest that they use their notebooks, drawing a picture if they like or jotting down a few words suggested by concentrating on one of the elements of the music. When the composition is over, they will then have a chance to voice their comments, exchanging ideas with classmates. Usually, as a child listens, he/she will concentrate on a single element. After exchanging ideas expressed in pictures or words, another listening may call for a different focus of attention and will be analyzed with different words or analogies. But the impetus to listen again properly comes from what has been discussed. When children are challenged by other children, they listen keenly and try to express their ideas in an original way.

Extending the Repertory

Soul, rhythm-and-blues, gospel, spirituals, folk blues, and pop songs are the backbone of children's listening fare. These songs never cease to be of prime interest. But once youngsters have acquired some techniques of perceptive listening with an improved vocabulary as a corollary, they will be receptive to other styles of instrumental compositions. If both the discussion about their music and the vocabulary they use to describe it has focused on certain basic concepts of musical composition (*beat* or *tempo*, *rhythmic character*, *volume* and *mood*), they will have a point of reference in listening to other works. In addition, boys and girls can find other compositions equally attractive. However, such compositions should be introduced after establishing a pattern of talking and writing about pop songs with as much precision as children can command.

Children's acceptance of other works will depend very much on the teacher's attitude about popular and composed music. A teacher cannot hold one style as superior to the other. Indeed, a cultivated musician appreciates what is of value in all music expression. When concert music is pulled down from its pedestal it can be genuinely enjoyed for itself or rejected as the case may be. No status is achieved by preferring "classical" music.

Some children may not widen their aural intake beyond pop music in spite of the impelling rhythms, exotic sounds, and superb performances in other works. A child has a right to his preferences; no value judgment should be placed on them by a teacher. But the compositions mentioned here and listed in the Discography—in a familiar musical idiom—have a fair chance of being accepted on their own merits and enjoyed by a majority of children. Interspacing different styles of music that are within the aural intake of an untrained listener not only adds variety but broadens the base for verbalizing.

Other factors being equal, the length of a piece has more to do with aural intake than style of composition. Children in grade school have a short attention span. For this reason, if a composition is long, play only one section, for playing time should not exceed that of a pop record. Records mentioned are banded to accommodate this.

Performances of a single work or section of a work can be repeated many times under different circumstances. Children absorb the sound without overt responses when it is played as a background to study or art work; they participate actively when music is played in Word Lab and also when it fills a pause between other activities. Sometimes it is wise to introduce a completely new sound when children are occupied in a quiet activity. In this way it has a ring of familiarity when repeated for attentive listening.

But attentive listening does not mean that children sit quietly with folded hands. Even adults are enjoying concerts in less formal ways in the last few years since dress and manners have become informal. The following is a quote from an article by Carman Moore that appeared in *Vogue* magazine the winter of 1971:

> In New York, attempts to do away with the traditional, padded-seat concert hall arrangement have been undertaken by the Whitney Museum of American Art. For a recent series, the Whitney audiences were seated on foam pillows on the floor. In another attempt, the Electric Circus gave walk-around concerts of electronic music and jazz (notably one by the Jazz Composers' Orchestra Association, Inc.).

Surely, children should be allowed the same informality.

Contemporary Composed Music

The musical culture of Afro-rooted children is extraordinarily rich—not only in the folk field where black musicians have been innovators of popular styles including blues, ragtime, improvised jazz, and rock, but also in the field of studied composition. It can safely be said that Afro-American musical practices have been the decisive factor in shaping *every* area of Western music in this century.[3]

3. Paul Henry Lang, *One Hundred Years of Music in America* (New York: G. Schirmer, Inc., 1961).

Since our avowed purpose is to build on the potential of black and Latin children through study of their own cultural resources, the main concentration here will be on contemporary works composed by blacks and Latins. Children should know that the music they are hearing is part of their ethnic heritage. However, an incidental mention of the fact with the title of the composition and name of the composer written on the board— a practice also used for pop music—is sufficient notice to give because a teacher does not want to set composed music apart from any other style.

Selections of contemporary music within children's attention span reach today's youngsters more than composed music of earlier periods. Contemporary works have the distinctive rhythms and sonorities of today, easier to identify with than the sound of another period. Since we are not concerned with the history of music, it is wise to choose those compositions to which children will be most responsive.

Suitable examples of contemporary music range wide from Afro-rooted drum compositions, composed jazz, African and Latin Masses, to concert music both instrumental and electronic. One or two albums from each of the categories furnish many short sections, ample to vary the diet of pop music.

Instrumental Jazz

One style of instrumental music easily accessible to grade-school children is jazz. Their ears are accustomed to the style since many soul songs have jazz accompaniments. When short sections of instrumental jazz are played purely for the pleasure of the sound, children usually respond enthusiastically (see Discography for selected titles).

The focus in jazz is on instruments magnificently played. As they listen to the performance of a lead instrument, boys and girls can apply what they learned in discussing pop music. Questions of tempo, rhythmic character, dynamics, and mood exploit the use of language.

Jazz brings up another topic for discussion, the *texture* of the music, which results from an interplay of instrumental parts. In an ensemble of, for example, drums, horn, bass, electric guitar and keyboard instruments, what kind of texture is created when they play together?

> Is it a rough texture like sandpaper or do the sounds blend together like honey?
>
> When a solo instrument takes the lead, does the texture change?
>
> What game do you play on the streets that comes to mind when you hear the drums? (Rat-a-tat-tat-tat)

Discussing a piece of music after listening not only develops language skills but also intensifies children's concentration on a replay. If his classmates hear something in the music that he has missed, he is likely to listen more keenly the next time for no child is impervious to the influence of other *children*.

A good book to have available on classroom shelves is *Journey into Jazz* by Nat Hentoff.[4] It is a forthright story about a boy who plays a trumpet. He tries again and again to join a group playing in a garage, but he is always sent back home to learn more until he discovers what jazz really means to those who play it—not an exercise demonstrating technical skill but a genuine expression of self.

Leaving album covers where children can look them over in free time often results in their asking to have the records they contain played in Word Lab. Attracted by pictures of people and/or instruments, they read titles; reading the titles leads them on to discover more in print. In this category of recordings with accompanying reading materials are two excellent histories of jazz tailored to the elementary level. Lang-

4. Nat Hentoff, *Journey into Jazz* (New York: Coward-McCann, Geoghan, 1968).

ston Hughes narrates *The Story of Jazz* [5] illustrating it with
selections by original performers as does "Cannonball" Adderly
in *A Child's Introduction to Jazz*.[6] The latter album has many
pictures of the instrumentalists going back as far as Scott Joplin,
"Jelly Roll" Morton, and Ma Rainey. Both albums have reading
materials for children whose interest is strong enough to want
to learn more about the subject. Don't play all of either album
at one time, however. A short portion to whet the appetite is
more intriguing than overindulgence.

Fusion of Folk and Art in Masses

Two recorded works, products of the ethnic heritage, that
are beautifully performed and beautifully packaged are *Misa
Criolla* by Ariel Ramirez,[7] a folk mass for soloists, chorus, and
orchestra, and *Missa Luba* by Ray Van Steen.[8] This latter work
is purely Congolese—"completely void of any modern western
musical influences." It is sung by a choir of 45 boys aged nine
to fourteen, aided by 15 teachers from the Kamua School. "Most
remarkable is the fact that none of the *Missa Luba* is written.
Certain rhythms, harmonies, and embellishments are spontaneous improvisations." Aside from any religious implications,
both these works are vital musical expressions that children
find exciting. Both recordings are banded to allow playing a
short, complete selection.

The albums that hold the records not only are good to
look at but also interesting for teacher or student to read. *Misa
Criolla* is sung in Spanish; the text is given in Spanish and
English.

5. *The Story of Jazz for Children*, narrated by Langston Hughes (Folkways Records).
6. *A Child's Introduction to Jazz*, narrated by "Cannonball" Adderly
(Wonderland Records).
7. Ariel Ramirez, *Misa Criolla* (Philips PCC 619).
8. Ray Van Steen, *Missa Luba* (Philips PCC 606).

Composed Music from Latin America

All children love the sound of percussion. They like to play percussion instruments and they like to hear them, especially in an ensemble of percussion only. Amadeo Roldán, a Cuban composer who lived early in this century, wrote a set of six pieces for percussion, called *Rítmicas*, the last two of which were recorded with *Three Cuban Dances* by George Russell and other short works by the white composers Cage, Cowell, and Harrison. The name of the record is *Concert Percussion for Orchestra*.[9] Spaced apart over a period of time, a single movement of these compositions adds interest and excitement to classroom listening.

Many works by other Latin-American composers have been recorded—Chavez, Ginastera, Villa-Lobos, and Guaneri, to mention the most famous. These are so generally attractive to children that selections of appropriate length are included in the recorded volumes of music basal texts and also in RCA's *Adventures in Music*.

A brief identification of the cultural setting of a composed work strengthens awareness that Latin-Americans and black Americans are making vital contributions in composed music as well as in popular music.

When children listen to such works, they follow the same procedure as when listening to folk or popular music: some may move to the music, others may write or draw in their notebooks, freely associating ideas the music suggests to them. If, in the course of discussion, one of the elements of music mentioned before is brought up naturally (beat, rhythm, volume, or mood) it can be pursued further—but not for the purpose of music instruction. The reason for directing attention to basic elements is to help children find verbal tools to express their genuine reactions to listening.

9. *Concert Percussion for Orchestra, Rítmicas* nos. 5 and 6 (Mainstream—MS 5011).

Composed Music Resonant of the
Black Experience

Just as children are more receptive to contemporary music
than to that of another period, so are they inclined to be more
receptive to composed works that are a product of their own
culture. For a composer's music is profoundly affected by his
own life experiences. Music not only reflects its time but, more
specifically, the particular environment in which it is composed.

Olly Wilson, a black composer, has said that there is a
unified cultural expression in the music of black people. Dr.
T. J. Anderson, also a black composer, used the term *inspired
intensity* to describe a characteristic that he believes is a unique
feature in the musical expression of all black people, composer
and nonmusician alike.

Children are tuned to the vibrations of their environment.
They respond to the *inspired intensity* of soul music and jazz
and can therefore more readily identify with this unique feature when they sense it in the works of black composers.

Two record albums that should be at hand in every urban
school are *The Black Composer in America*, played by the
Oakland Youth Orchestra,[10] and *Natalie Hinderas Plays Music
by Black Composers*,[11] which is a two-record album of piano
music. Both albums are made up of short works which, of
course, should be introduced individually from time to time to
attract attention by the very contrast they furnish to the usual
listening repertory. (Other recordings by black composers are
listed in the Discography, Appendix II.)

10. *The Black Composer in America*, played by the Oakland Youth
Orchestra, Robert Hughes, Conductor (Desto Records—DC 7107). See Discography for selections.
11. *Natalie Hinderas Plays Music by Black Composers* (Desto Records
—DC 7102/3). See Discography for selections.

Electronic Music

The ears of children who live in the space age are also receptive to electronic music. Composers of such works have freed sound from the restraints of orchestral instruments— which are limited in range of melody—and also of performers, who are humanly incapable of playing the complex rhythms that can be achieved electronically.

A great diversity of sound is possible through electronic means. For example, electronics can produce pitch far above and below the conventional range as well as synthesized rhythms that suggest the assymetrical patterns of African drumming. Basic concepts of musical composition, nevertheless, still apply. Children can recognize in electronic works the elements of tempo, as it relates to their own experiences, the dynamics, mood, texture, and overall rhythmic character. They can express their reactions in more vivid language than many adults who know only that they "can't stand that racket."

A sneak performance of electronic music (when children are quietly busy) has real shock value. It will open eyes and ears, turning some children on, some children off. But it will make an impression that can be verbalized in discussions.

An instructive record, *Sounds of New Music* (Folkways), includes works by Cage, Varese, and Cowell, well known for their unconventional use of instruments, as well as electronic compositions by Ussachevsky, Luening, El-Dabh, and others. This recording furnishes examples of repertory suitable for class listening and also written material about electronic music for students interested enough to read about the subject in depth.

At the present writing both black and white composers are combining the natural media (instruments and voices) with the electronic medium. One example is a tape-transformed voice and instrumental composition by Halim El-Dabh, *Leiyla and the Poet* (Columbia MS 6566). Another by Olly Wilson is *Piano Piece*, piano and electronic sounds, which is one of the selections on the Natalie Hinderas recording mentioned above.

Individual Preferences

Hearing a great variety of music with the wide spectrum of sound that is used today—from soul to electronic music—is a broadening experience for children. If the practice is continued over a whole year with examples of different styles, some aspect of music will reach every child—will arouse his interest, stir him to articulate his preferences for certain types and selections of composition, and give him the courage and the experience to make an independent judgment. Time is well spent in playing all kinds of music. An internal, personal experience is externalized, total perception is increased, and boys and girls enrich their vocabulary in talking about music they want to hear.

Children Make Music

Throughout this book, I have suggested that children need little direction to improvise an instrumental background either to accompany the reading of poetry or prose or to supply music for a dramatic performance. I take this stand with the firm belief that children who choose to make such a contribution to a joint project will achieve results satisfying to themselves and their classmates. For the naturally musical child who is not preoccupied with the technical demands of fingering an instrument or reading a score is sensitive to the mood of whatever she/he is accompanying and also perceptive of its tempo, rhythmic character, and dynamic qualities. These are basic characteristics of musical instinct inherent—in different degrees—in the makeup of the trained and untrained instrumentalist.

My belief in children's natural ability was affirmed in the 1960s when great numbers of teen-agers taught themselves to play instruments in order to form their own rock bands. Boys, especially, half-hearted in response to their music programs at school, applied themselves with diligence, enthusiasm, and energy, much to the bewilderment of their teachers. Left to their own resources, the aspiring performers found release for their natural bent toward music-making with a driving will to accomplish something pleasing to themselves.

All children in a class can become personally involved with music-making. The musical concepts that focused their attention in listening to composed music will help them in what they want to accomplish. Such a project is not isolated from language development because to gain their ends they are obliged to clarify their thinking and make their plans through verbal exchanges and to project their ideas to others in writing and diagraming.

Improvising on the percussion instruments normally found in the classroom allows for free expression of a child's natural feeling for music. For this reason, children throughout the grades begin making music by playing a wide variety of percussion instruments but also by striking, scratching, or stroking nonmusical objects at hand, and by using voice, hands, and feet to create pure sound.

In planning to improvise a composition without the frame of spoken words—an improvisation that is a purely musical design—a time limitation can supply the boundaries. The improvisation should be of short duration—under a minute, timed by a stopwatch, desk or wall clock. Children discuss before they start whether it shall begin quietly or with a bang (dynamics), in what tempo it shall move, whether it shall be smooth or highly syncopated (rhythmic character), what instrumentation shall be used (texture), to convey what mood.

Once begun from complete silence, children *feel* their way to the closing because the agreed-upon decisions at the beginning more or less determine the general character of the piece. For example, if a group decides to open with a crash of cymbals, or ring of a triangle, players may "sneak in" tentatively under the continuing sound with contrasting sonorous material *in a free rhythm*. Allowing their musical instinct to direct them, they add a knock, a sharp or grating sound in counterpoint to the lasting vibrations of the cymbal or triangle. What follows develops freely from this beginning. On the other hand, if a piece is opened with sand blocks, vocal noises, or clicking sounds on a *steady beat*, it is likely that the beat will be maintained by the other participants with only occasional offbeat sounds as accents.

In the same way, a loud beginning may be followed with a sudden drop in dynamic level to be increased slowly to a climax or to a smashing finish or the excitement of the sound may be sustained to the very end.

Each child plays as if he were on a team, intuitively sensing musical concepts as they apply without conscious thought after the preliminary decisions. He instinctively knows when a particular sound strengthens the composition, how long to continue it and when to let it go. Given free reign, the natural musicality of children takes over and allows them to function in a manner commensurate with their degree of coordination and experience.

If expectations are high for a group—no matter what their age—they perform remarkably sensitively, responding to group dynamics in a natural but intensely concentrated way. If a teacher is skeptical of their seriousness of purpose, however, children sense this as well, kid around a lot, and finally blow the whole thing.

When children work together in a creative effort, their interest can be sustained by expecting them to reach higher. A tape recorder proves a valuable aid for self-evaluation. It is thrilling to hear the replay of what you have done, to discuss how it can be redone to sound better or, if reasonably satisfied, how to improvise a contrasting section. Little by little a sonorous picture is developed, embodying basic musical elements.

Children in the upper grades go further in their experiments with the tape machine or cassette. Although the substance of their improvisation is still percussion, solo instruments that children are studying might be added to the ensemble.

After starting in much the same way as younger children, they explore the possibilities of replaying their improvisation at a slower or faster speed than that at which it was recorded. "Are parts of it more effective at a different tempo?" They listen to how tempo and volume affect the sound of particular instruments. "Is it worth another try to play one of the instruments louder or softer?"

It is exciting, too, to hear the replay backward, like viewing one's painting, drawing or handwriting in a mirror. Such experiments, which are real attention-getters, increase children's awareness of the numerous possibilities of tone and sound manipulation. Ears are sharpened to become more appreciative of what contemporary composers are achieving in sound-oriented compositions.

Such elementary experiments may well provide an incentive for more intensive work in this area by a student particularly interested in music and electronics. His attention should be called to additional available information. Most of the music textbook series for elementary grades treat the subject of electronic composition in the sixth-grade book. There is also a booklet on electronic music issued as a reprint of the November 1968 issue of the *Music Educators Journal*.[12]

Increased awareness of the nuances of sound helps children's speech when teachers draw on their potential for acute hearing in learning oral English. The awakening of aesthetic sensitivity promotes other objectives as well—the forming of positive attitudes, the will and energy to communicate with others, the desire to know more about a subject of interest, and the conviction that basic skills must be mastered to accomplish one's purpose. Objectives are rarely achieved in isolation; the interaction with one another leads toward total development of personality as well as progress in academic learning.

12. *Music Educators Journal* (MENC), Center for Educational Associations, Reston, Va.

Community Aids

Music is a strong tie between the community and the school. Ask children to invite an instrumentalist or vocalist they know to perform for the class or for an assembly of several classes. Have the children invite their parents to such an occasion and make sure that the guest speaks to the class after his performance. Children like live music; they like to see and touch the instruments and ask a dozen questions of the performer.

Teachers of several classes can get together to request the administration to arrange for one or more Young Audience Concerts.[13] This is an enriching experience for children that stimulates activity in many areas of curriculum.

In between visits of outsiders, have older children play for younger children and boys or girls who are studying instruments play for their class. Far better than taking a class to a concert hall is to encourage them to give a concert in school for classmates and friends. They should write "program notes" for the selection they choose to play, a sentence or two which different children read aloud as an introduction.

Rewarding music experiences can often be integrated into the school schedule without borrowing time from other subjects. In some schools, the day is always started with music to make a smooth transition from the outside world to the classroom. Such a beginning of the class day ideally can prepare children to work more productively. This is the time for psychological adjustment. The few minutes it takes to play a selection is slight compared to its effect on children.

From time to time the whole period of Word Lab can be given over to music. An active listening experience that includes reading and writing as corrollaries may be the one experience that lights up a child who is unresponsive. Music makes a

13. Young Audiences, Inc., 115 East 92d Street, New York, N.Y. 10028.

powerful appeal to children. It is almost sure to arouse their interest and hold their attention.

Individual and team research projects motivated by collective experiences are properly carried out in the supplementary periods usually with the intent of feeding material back into the lab period.

Some listening experiences might occur simultaneously with other studies, as a background to them; some fill the inevitable and often awkward pauses in class routines; others are used purely as creative recreation. The accumulative effect of many such experiences makes it worthwhile for a teacher to turn to music as an aid in enriching the classroom environment.

Learn to Read/Read to Learn

9

Lest we forget or be diverted by attractive materials and activities, it should be mentioned again that our main target is that children learn to read. This is a goal a teacher constantly keeps in mind. Each experience that has been introduced has this goal as an objective.

Children, however, have different goals every day. Stressing to them the importance of learning to read makes little positive impression and often causes anxiety, for future rewards of learning seem too distant an objective to realize. Children's objectives must be in sight. They dedicate their energy to the daily *doing,* to an engaging project at hand. Each project holds its own reward in the satisfaction of doing it well according to their own lights.

A teacher sees further. A teacher can see how individual children make progress through well-planned experiences: how one child gains deeper insight into a problem; how another learns a new word to use; how a third takes interest in a book for the first time and makes an attempt to read it; how a shy child gradually opens up and is able to assume leadership in a study group or in Word Lab. Each one moves forward at his own pace, not all with giant steps—after all, some children's legs are shorter than others—but each child moves forward from the spot under his feet.

Little is gained by mapping out the whole journey in advance, but a child can be encouraged to get on the way through many daily experiences he/she enjoys with classmates. When learning is induced, and the habit of using what one learns becomes a daily practice, children read because they want to read. They want to read because they have glimpsed the pleasurable part of reading; the fascination of finding people like themselves in books, the excitement caused by hearing events recounted, the stimulation of thinking and feeling that results from identification with the thoughts and feelings of others.

Children get close to books through diversified experiences that take into account their maturity and life style. Students of minority cultures in particular gain insight into their own strength and achieve confidence through work in multi-art media. This statement was attested to by hundreds of teachers interviewed for a national survey entitled *The Arts, Education, and the Urban Sub-Culture.*[1] The point was made over and over again by teachers in schools that the opportunity to learn

---

1. Don D. Bushnell and Kathi Corbera Bushnell, *The Arts, Education, and the Urban Sub-Culture,* Communications Foundation, 2020 Alameda Padre Serra, Santa Barbara, Calif. 93103. 1969.

through expressive arts intensifies children's *will* to learn which, applied to academic studies, shows positive results.

When children are surrounded by books, by record albums, by pictures, word charts, and students' written reports—the contents of which they learn about in Word Lab—they turn to these resources to research what they need to know. Each child satisfies the need according to his/her state of development at the moment. But as confidence grows, each child progressively tackles a more challenging problem of decoding to help realize a class objective.

End-of-School Program

Throughout this book we have been discussing how the literature, traditional and contemporary, of Afro-rooted cultures serves as an inspiring force for improvised speech, miming, dance, art, and music; and what is pertinent here, how the collective experiences made possible through a study of this literature lead children to read and write. The subject to be dealt with here is how these techniques can be reinforced by an end-of-year program to result in an effective recall of the year's work.

The idea for a program evolves gradually, almost spontaneously, as the culmination of weeks of study. It is not a goal to begin with. Throughout the year boys and girls become deeply involved in content of absorbing materials. They view their work from many angles, studying bits and pieces, interpreting themes, phrases, and words in ways they find stimulating. Technical study of reading and writing, through phonetics and by learning to recognize whole words and sentences, goes along then with personal expressiveness.

When children work in this way with a quantity of poetry and prose, favorite subjects are called for again and again. One of the favorite subjects that has been studied may be in the category of proverb or parable, ballad or fable, heroic legend, or historical material, contemporary poetry or children's books. Or it may come from something a child has read or heard and brought to the attention of other members of the class. In any case, if further study is to be creative, the material must offer possibilities for greater exploration, for study in depth.

In a Second-Grade Word Lab

The specific studies that led to an end-of-year program for children in a second grade started with the difficulty of pronouncing a name. Interest was aroused by a child from Puerto Rico telling the highlights of a story she heard folklorist Pura Belpré read aloud in the New York Public Library. The folk tale is about an old witch who meets José in the woods. The witch takes José to her house and keeps him there until he can guess her name. As he goes about chores she gives him to do, he asks a cow, a goat, and a pig to help him guess her name. They all refuse, but finally an oversized crab tells him "Her name is *Casi Lampu'a Lentemué*." For children who do not speak Spanish, that is a difficult name to pronounce but for those who do, Casi Lampu'a Lentemué rolls off the tongue in a flowing rhythm.

The idea of guessing a name—and one as difficult as that— fascinated children. A synopsis of the story [2] was read aloud and everyone practiced the name. It was written on the board, the rhythm of its syllables analyzed (short short short long— short short long). Children played with the syllables in sing-song speech. One group represented it in percussive sounds on body, on objects in the room and on drum; another with dancing steps; a single child sang the name repeating it three times in a melody of a few tones spontaneously made up. Every member of the class was clamoring for a turn to do it his/her

2. "Casi Lampu'a Lentemué" is printed in its entirety in *Making Music Your Own*, Book 2 (Morristown, N.J.: Silver Burdett, 1971). Children can follow the story by looking at illustrations, succinctly titled.

way. In short order, all the children were on intimate terms with the sound of Casi Lampu'a Lentemué and various representations of it. Some children's diction was bolstered by sight, others by sound, still others by movement. But each found a clue to successful performance.

This kind of play continued with words and phrases that are repeated in each sequence of the story. Children learned to recognize repeated phrases and to identify the name Casi Lampu'a Lentemué in a list of words, from a rhythm beat out on a drum, from the tune for her name, and from steps in movement that symbolized it.

Children became so involved in this story, the teacher realized it could be developed further. As a research project the class took a trip to the zoo to notice especially the domestic animals who had a part in the story. Back in the classroom, some chose to imitate the way each creature moved; others approximated the sounds they made. A few children decided to make up a tune of short compass on a xylophone as a leitmotif for other characters in the story.

Second-Grade Fiesta

Work in Word Lab continued as usual with many other examples of folklore and contemporary writing. But the children often looked at illustrations of Casi in their books, read titles of the pictures and asked to hear again the story of Casi Lampu'a Lentemué. When the prospect of dramatizing a subject for a fiesta came up, one of the first mentioned was the Puerto Rican story. Several other titles of works children suggested were written on the board and a secret ballot was taken. The vote was overwhelmingly for Casi.

Each child was given a copy of a shortened version of the story. The class discussed how it could be divided into scenes and meticulously drew lines on their script between them. Then scenes were labeled with the words *Introduction, Scene I*, etc.

The whole group started work on a dance-drama. They started by forming a large circle to work out the meaning of each scene. No parts were assigned; anyone who had an idea for action of one of the characters stepped inside the circle and offered an interpretation. Children forming the circle snapped fingers, clapped hands, and made foot and mouth noises to give a setting.

Each sequence was developed as a separate unit and gradually defined after innumerable improvisations in speech and action of individual children within the circle. The others repeated the actions and were thus qualified to judge which were the best to adopt. Chorus parts evolved almost spontaneously as they related to the action within the circle. At no time did the teacher put words in children's mouths or suggest style of movement or particular steps.

Thus all children shared in the experience of bringing the typed script to life, each taking part in his chosen way to make the recognized words meaningful. While performance was taking shape, some children worked in art on masks for heads of animals and for characteristic clothing for the witch. Others worked out musical motifs for the characters. Beyond this, all the music they wanted was animal noises and self-made percussive sounds.

The final action took place in the open part of a semicircle. Characters who mimed the action changed for each scene as did the narrator who stood at the side. Those in the semicircle were both the vocal and dance chorus, each child functioning as an individual yet sensitively aware of the contribution he or she was making to the whole.

There was no last-minute pressure for learning or rehearsing parts. It was not a performance in the conventional way that performances are usually put together toward the end of a school year but was more precisely a demonstration of the study that had been going on daily in the classroom. Because individual parts had been created by the children themselves, every child knew what to do. They refined their knowledge in the field they had chosen and reinforced their learning through expressive performance. An important part of this learning was learning how to function in relation to each other.

Integration of Learning in Upper Grades

In the upper grades, as in the lower grades, the literature boys and girls have studied during the school year is reviewed in order to choose certain favorites for an end-of-year program. As an example, let's say that a slow reader in the fifth or sixth grade had been attracted by a poem in the anthology *Beyond the Blues, New Poems by American Negroes*.[3] We will suppose that the title of the book first caught his attention. As he thumbed it through, he found a poem of short lines and repeated words, called "Charles Parker, 1925–1955." He was attracted by the name. "I can decode that," he reasoned and thought of the glory it would shed upon him when he read it aloud in Word Lab. If his best friend would help him out he might even win the poetry-reading contest for the month (see p. 142).

This is the poem our slow reader made the effort to decipher:

Charles Parker, 1925–1955
WARING CUNEY

Listen,
This here
Is what
Charlie
Did
To the Blues.
Listen,
That there

3. *Beyond the Blues, New Poems by American Negroes*, selected and introduced by Rosey Pool. First published in England by the Hand and Flower Press, Lympne Hythe Kent, and distributed in this country by Dufour Editions, Inc., Chester Springs, Pa. 1962.

Is what
Charlie
Did
To the Blues.
This here,
bid-dle-dee-dee
bid-dle-dee-dee
bopsheep
have you any cool?
bahdada
one horn full.
Charlie
Filled the Blues
With
Curly-cues.
That's What
Charlie
Did
To the Blues.
Play
That again
Drop
A nickel in,
Charlie's
Dead,
Charlie's
Gone,
But
John Burkes
Carried on.
Drop
A nickel in,
Give
The platter
A spin,
Let's listen
To what
Charlie
Did
To the Blues.

I can imagine the enthusiasm such a poem would generate in Word Lab and again, in review, for it sounds like a talking blues, a form most children respond to with enthusiasm.

Those who have analyzed classic blues, listened to blues, sung or spoken a blues, and made up a talking blues, would be familiar with the form, also, with the character of improvisations that fill the pause at the end of lines. But they would probably need help to discover that several short lines of the poem as printed, differing in number, make up one blues line. What gives the clue? Each full blues line is marked by a period at the end. (A lesson in punctuation.) So, in spite of the free form and the design on the page, the poem can be studied as a talking blues.

To do this, children as individuals or in teams would rewrite the poem in blues lines. If a child makes a *personal* copy of a contemporary poem for his own use, copyright laws are not infringed, whereas a teacher may not duplicate the poem for class use without permission of the copyright owners.

Studying one line of their copy at a time, children would discover that the second blues line repeats the first with slight variations. That is also what they would expect because of previous experience with the blues form. The third line is a play of words on "Baa Baa Black Sheep." That is fun to discover and fun to play with vocally in order to embellish the line. This third line might be considered as the end of a stanza, the completion of a thought. Holding that idea in reserve, boys and girls would go on to the next blues lines.

The next two lines as defined by periods are very short; they give time for elaborate improvisation to fill the pauses after them. How can you make *curly-cues* with the voice? Both lines are related as are the first two of the poem. And then, if the poem is rewritten in blues lines, someone would notice that there are *two* lines remaining—two long lines—making four for this verse instead of three lines as in the first. The fourth line is again a variation of the previous one and could be considered a collective improvisation on the solo that preceded it.

Some children would probably notice the reference to play-ing a jukebox with a nickel and would certainly point out that a jukebox today costs more than a nickel. Back they would go to the source to read the biographical notes that precede the poem in order to find out how long ago the poem was written.

If this poem were chosen for an end-of-school program to be performed as a talking blues, it would call for a musical background throughout, possibly made up of drums, guitar, and horn, if one of the boys or girls played a horn. Or a music committee might find an instrumental blues recording appro-priate to play as a background. Whoever played the tape or record player would have an important part, too, adjusting the volume of the music to the texture and volume of the voice parts.

In addition, there are other ways for children to demon-strate their reading comprehension of this poem. Those who know the style of soul-music singing groups might suggest adding choreography. Boys and girls who have watched such groups as The Temptations, The Jackson Five, or The Staple Singers live or on TV know how members of the group sup-port the soloist by acting out lyrics as the words are being sung. Several youngsters who favor movement as their mode of expression could form a group and work out their chore-ography to relate it to the poem.

If such a program were to take place in a classroom, can you imagine the satisfaction and joy of the child who originally found the poem? His self-confidence and esteem would rise in direct proportion to the level of his reading ability. The antholo-gies of folklore and contemporary literature mentioned in the Bibliography have a plentiful number of examples of both poetry and prose that are similarly simple to read but chal-lenging in possibilities for interpretation.

Suggest that children review the poems and short prose works they have studied during the year to see which ones hold possibilities for dramatizations, for adding vocal and move-ment choruses, and for instrumental music, live or recorded—

in short for collective presentation that involves the whole class. This kind of planning entails rereading, analyzing, digging for meaning in order to interpret words in other media. When an immediate goal of end-of-school program is in sight, children's energy can be directed into productive channels.

Arranging a Program of Creative Writings

A recap of several pieces of original writing should also be considered by the class as appropriate material for an end-of-school program. The opportunity to review this material promotes reading to the same degree as other works do and at once places high value on creative writing.

Such a program might take the form of a variety show with several unrelated demonstrations of classwork (of which there are many examples throughout these pages). These would be accompanied by music and dance and possibly alternated with recorded music. Children would be asked to look through their notebooks and bring anything they considered pertinent to read aloud in Word Lab. Those pieces that the class found interesting would be duplicated for everyone to study.

To enliven the project teachers should help children choose material with several considerations in mind:

> Can a few lines of refrain be spoken by a vocal chorus to introduce each composition thus dividing the program into sections?
>
> Do the pieces suggest a percussive or instrumental background or interlude?
>
> Can some of them be interpreted in movement by a repeated routine that a group devises or by free movement of individuals (as in "Casi")?

In short, pieces of original composition would be treated in much the same way as children had learned to interpret other written material.

Another possibility for a program on a larger scale is to choose several pieces of original writings on a particular subject. The same criteria as above would apply in making final choices with an additional consideration:

> Can a narrative or dialogue be written or improvised to act as a connecting link between the loosely related pieces?

Listening to a recording of a musical show called *The Me Nobody Knows* [4] might inspire such a treatment. The spoken text was written by children between the ages of seven and eighteen attending schools in underprivileged neighborhoods of New York City. Lyrics, also written by children, were woven into the fabric of the play which was in addition performed by young people in the same age range.

Another model for an end-of-school program is described in chapter 7 on p. 151 ("Drama of Identity"). In that, a dance-drama was made up from the compositions of several children in a Trinidad school who wrote about a hurricane they experienced.

Review to Promote Reading Skills

Reviewing familiar materials often throws new light upon them. Problems of reading or comprehension that attended the first effort are usually lessened when the same material is introduced later in the term. Not only has children's reading ability improved over the year, but they have less anxiety in approaching familiar material.

For example, poor readers who are drawn into a collective experience by interesting subject matter introduced in Word Lab are often carried along by more able readers. But if they have had an opportunity to participate successfully in inter-

4. *The Me Nobody Knows* (Atlantic S-1566).

preting the subject matter that is represented in words, they have gotten close to the material in a way that was possible for them at the time.

When the material is reviewed, children play different roles than in the earlier interpretations. The boy or girl who supplied music may have the courage to try a narrative part, or one who took part in a chorus of dancers might feel confident enough to do research for a project. Changing roles not only for characters of a dramatization but for those other contributions that enliven and enrich a class project allows children different ways to interpret the printed word and at once affords each individual a chance for reading functionally.

The values of summing up the year's work in preparing for an end-of-school program are manifold. Preparations entail further research, reading, analyzing, discussing, organizing materials, and, in some instances, creating physical props as well as working out a dramatic conception. Such a program also includes writing, listening, speaking, and the experience of working with others in artistic expression. It is not only a review of what children have studied but also a new application of the techniques they have learned.

Once children learn basic skills of reading and writing, they are equipped to devote themselves to other subjects of the curriculum with a stronger degree of confidence and purpose gained through expressive arts. Those who have daily practice in reading functionally in order to find out *what they want to know* set themselves a dynamic precedent. They can transfer the skill as needed to other areas of study. A writer in an educational book of the 1960s made an apt analogy: If a child lights up in one subject of curriculum, there is good chance he can come alive across the board.

APPENDIX I

Annotated Bibliography

For practical purposes this is an abridged bibliography. It includes only those books that relate directly to the thesis of this book and augment its material. All books listed are easy to come by either for perusal in local libraries or through inexpensive purchase from the publisher.

For those teachers who wish to pursue a particular subject further, many of the books entered here have extensive bibliographies. In addition, sources for available material are cited.

Philosophy of Education

From myriad books on education, the following minimal number (listed in order of publication) are chosen to represent five viewpoints on the educative process:

Viewpoint of Scientists

Jerome S. Bruner. *The Process of Education*. Cambridge, Mass.: Harvard University Press, 1960.

A report of a conference held at Woods Hole, Massachusetts, in 1959 under the auspices of the National Academy of Sciences, was published in book form by its chairman, Jerome S. Bruner. The conclusion reached by leading scholars and educators attending the conference outlined a philosophy of education that has affected the thinking of teachers in every discipline.

An important thesis is that learning and teaching are more effective when the fundamental structure of material is presented in a form children can apprehend *intuitively*. Instruction then builds upon their intuitive understanding.

Organic Teaching

Sylvia Ashton-Warner. *Teacher*. New York: Simon & Schuster, 1963.

A highly readable account of a practicing teacher's experience with Maori children in New Zealand demonstrates "organic" teaching, that is, releasing the native imagery of the child and using it for working material.

Sylvia Ashton-Warner also has a 1973 book, *Spearpoint*, *"Teacher"* in America (New York: Alfred A. Knopf), which points up effects of American society on its children.

Psychosocial Research

Eleanor Burke Leacock. *Teaching and Learning in City Schools*. New York: Basic Books, 1969.

The second book of *Psychosocial Studies in Education* from the Research Division, Bank Street College of Education, deals with factors that contribute to the obvious "miseducation" received by many pupils, especially by children who are poor and black. Through a comparative study of classrooms, pupils, and teachers, by a research team, the author makes clear how the attitudes and values of teachers help to mold a child's opinion of himself and his response to the educative process.

Cultural Understanding: Learning Through Literature

Karel Rose. *A Gift of the Spirit: Readings in Black Literature for Teachers.* New York: Holt, Rinehart & Winston, 1971. Paperback.

The first part of the book introduces Imaginative Literature as a way of Knowing, followed by practical guidance for teachers in finding sources of black literature and valuable criteria for choosing works that present a broad spectrum of Negro life.

The literary works in the second section have been chosen by the author in consultation with a board of ten Negro educators. The selections are arranged in chapters according to themes, prefaced with the author's text and questions for discussion, and followed by summaries and supplementary references. A wide range of reading materials are referred to throughout the book as well as listed in an extensive bibliography.

A Gift of the Spirit does more however than expand knowledge of black reading materials. In the author's words: "My major concern is with what literature can do to increase sensitivity, and my intent is to utilize the aesthetic medium for heightening awareness in the literary way of knowing."

Natural Learning

Herbert Kohl. *Reading, How To, A People's Guide to Alternative Methods of Learning and Testing.* New York: E. P. Dutton & Co., Inc., 1973.

Kohl believes that under favorable circumstances people of any age can acquire the skill of reading in a natural and informal manner—as they learn to walk or talk. Skill is developed through collective reading aloud by students on various levels cooperating with each other. Interruptions for language play and for discussion of pertinent issues that rise from the text are an integral part of the reading session.

This is a valuable book for teachers because Kohl supports his view with practical suggestions of materials and procedures, including a succinct chart of basic phonetic sounds.

Anthologies of Folklore

The Black Experience in United States

The Book of Negro Folklore. Edited by Langston Hughes and Arna Bontemps. New York: Dodd, Mead, 1958.

The single most comprehensive folk anthology of the cultural contributions made by the Negro people in the United States. It abounds with representative selections of folklore ranging from antebellum days to the present, originating on the plantation and the levee, in Old New Orleans, Chicago, and Harlem. Included are animal tales and rhymes, games, spirituals and blues, sermons and slave memories as well as modern gospel songs, jazz and jive, poetry and prose in the folk manner by leading black writers and lyricists. A book children as well as teachers can use profitably.

Bessie Jones and Bess Lomax Hawes. *Step It Down: Games, Plays, Songs and Stories from the Afro-American Heritage.* New York: Harper & Row, 1972.

An abundance of materials for children throws light on learning through play. The informal text gives a teacher a profound insight into traditional values of the Afro-American heritage.

A selected bibliography of more than fifty works related to the materials is presented for further investigation of the subject.

Additional Sources of Enrichment

Ain't You Got a Right to the Tree of Life? The People of Johns Island, South Carolina, Their Faces, Their Words, and Their Songs. Recorded by Guy and Candy Carawan. Photographed by Robert Yellin. New York: Simon & Schuster, 1967.

The photographs and words of people as they speak and sing of their past and present in a rural community convey a sense of history to children more vividly than anything that could be written *about* people.

Harold Courlander. *Negro Folk Music U.S.A.* New York and London: Columbia University Press, 1963.

An illuminating text relates historical and organic development to social setting and traditions. For students' research it includes examples of spirituals, work songs, blues, ring games, creole songs, songs of social comment, of complaint, and others.

Collections of Folklore Verses

Afro-America Sings. Prepared by a Detroit Public Schools Workshop under the direction of Ollie McFarland. Publication 4-614 TXT, The Board of Education of the School District of the City of Detroit. 1971.

Alan Lomax. *The Folk Songs of North America,* Part IV: *The Negro South.* Garden City, N.Y.: Doubleday, 1960.

Beatrice Landeck. *"Git on Board."* Collection of Folk Songs. New York: Edward B. Marks, 1964.

Beatrice Landeck and Elizabeth Crook. *Wake Up and Sing.* New York: Marks/Morrow, 1969.

Beatrice Landeck. *Echoes of Africa in Folk Songs of the Americas.* New York: David McKay Company, Inc., 1969.

The Black Experience in Latin America

Wilfred G. Cartey. *Black Images.* New York: Teachers College Press of Columbia University, 1970.

One of the publications of the Center for Education in Latin America: Institute of International Studies. Traces the literary evolution of the black man from the image of slave to one of human distinction. It covers differing manifestations of the black man's image in parts of the Caribbean, in South America, and in the United States, with text for teachers and numerous examples of poetic expression for students' research. Those in Spanish and French are given literal translation in English.

Frances Toor. *A Treasury of Mexican Folkways.* New York: Crown Publishers, 1947.

A definitive research work describing the customs, myths, folklore, traditions, beliefs, fiestas, dances and songs of the Mexican people. The text will be of interest to teachers who might direct students to specific examples (in English translation) and to numerous drawings and photographs.

Collections of Folklore Verses with Latin American Examples

Renadio del Cantar Folklórico de Puerto Rico, compiled by Monserrate Deliz. San Juan, Puerto Rico: Universidad de Puerto Rico, 1951. Paperback.

Beatrice Landeck. *Echoes of Africa in Folk Songs of the Americas.* New York: David McKay Company, Inc., 1969.

Francisco López Cruz. *La Música Folklórica de Puerto Rico.* Sharon, Conn.: Troutman Press, 1967.

El Toro Pinto and Other Songs in Spanish, selected and illustrated by Anne Rockwell. New York: Macmillan, 1971.

Songs Belafonte Sings. New York: Duell, Sloan & Pearce, 1962.

The Black Experience in Africa

An African Treasury. Selected by Langston Hughes. New York: Crown Publishers, 1960. Also available in paperback from Pyramid Books, 444 Madison Avenue, New York, N.Y. 10022. Articles/essays/stories/poems by black Africans.

A popular sampling of writing selected by Langston Hughes from floods of material he received in response to announcements in local newspapers in many parts of Africa. The wide range of subject matter reflects the varied backgrounds of the writers. Many of the short stories, read aloud, will interest children.

Collections of Folklore Verses with African Examples

William I. Kaufman, *UNICEF Book of Children's Songs.* Harrisburg, Pa.: Stackpole Books, 1970.

Mosche Sephula. *Sing, Africa!* and *Sing Again, Africa!* Folios. Gaillard Limited, 1970. Available from Galaxy Music Corporation, 2121 Broadway, N.Y. 10023.

English translations of African lyrics can also be found in sections of *Afro-America Sings* and *Echoes of Africa*.

Anthologies of Contemporary Literature

Reference Books for Teachers and for Students' Research

Karel Rose. *A Gift of the Spirit: Readings in Black Literature for Teachers.* New York: Holt, Rinehart & Winston, 1971. Paperback.

An extraordinarily thorough source book. Annotated in first section of Bibliography, Philosophy of Education.

Beyond the Blues: New Poems by American Negroes. Selected and introduced by Rosey Pool. Chester Springs, Pa.: Dufour Editions, 1962.

A unique collection of "contemporary voices" by "some fifty different men and women of varying ages: seventeen to ninety-four, in different styles, different rhythms, different moods, from widely differing states of mind." Biographical notes on each poet and a most interesting 20-page introduction for a teacher. Many poems for reading aloud and students' research.

Black on Black. Edited by Arnold Adoff. New York: Collier Books, 1970. Paperback.

Commentaries by Black Americans from Frederick Douglass to Malcolm X.

Dark Symphony, Negro Literature in America. Edited by James A. Emanual and Theodore L. Gross. New York: Free Press, 1968. Paperback.

A source book presenting a comprehensive survey of black writing in the nineteenth and twentieth centuries from Frederick Douglass to works in prose and poetry by major living writers. The introduction, text throughout the book, and biographies that preface an author's work make this an unusually valuable source book for the library. An extensive bibliography includes a listing of the published works of each of the authors.

I Am the Darker Brother: An Anthology of Modern Poems by Black Americans. Edited by Arnold Adoff. New York: Collier Books, 1970. Paperback.

A useful, inexpensive introduction to the works of modern black poets with an inspiring foreword by Charlemae Rollins. She tells how browsing through a book of poems may lead a child to other books and other poems and possibly to becoming a writer of poetry and prose.

The Poetry of the Negro 1746–1970. Edited by Langston Hughes and Arna Bontemps. New York: Doubleday, 1970.

A classic anthology including the works of 163 Negro poets from pre-Revolutionary times to the present. The representative selection of poems of moderns from Paul Lawrence Dunbar, James Weldon Johnson, Claude McKay, Jean Toomer, Countee Cullen and the compilers to Gwendolyn Brooks, LeRoi Jones, and Ishmael Reed serves to introduce the reader to individual writers whose complete works are available in published collections.

A shorter second section called "Tributary Poems" assembles works by white poets who have been inspired to write about the black experience in the Western world.

3000 Years of Black Poetry: An Anthology. Edited by Alan Lomax and Raoul Abdul. New York: Dodd, Mead, 1970.

Poems by black poets of all times and all nations from the black kings of ancient Egypt to the Africans and Afro-Americans of today. Each category is prefaced by text. A source of riches for the classroom.

Anthologies of Children's Poetry

The Me Nobody Knows, Children's Voices from the Ghetto. Edited by Stephen M. Joseph. New York: Avon Books, 1972. Paperback.

William I. Kaufman. *UNICEF Book of Children's Poems*. Harrisburg, Pa.: Stackpole Books, 1970.

The Voice of the Children. Collected by June Jordan and Terri Bush. New York: Holt, Rinehart & Winston, 1970.

Kenneth Koch. *Wishes, Lies and Dreams*. New York: Random House, 1970. Paperback.

Kenneth Koch. *Rose, Where Did You Get That Red?* New York: Random House, 1973.

Collections of Folk Tales

All books are well illustrated and are set in readable type. Most of the collections are from one major locality but the following has selections from four Third World areas:

Third World Voices for Children. Edited by Robert E. McDowell and Edward Lavitt. New York: The Third World Press—Joseph Okpaku Publishing, 1971.

Stories from Africa, West Indies, United States, and New Guinea with a description of the location as an introduction to each section. Some stories combine realism and magic; others are purely realistic. Written in fictional style, their subject matter and appeal are to upper grades.

From Africa

African Folktales. Edited by Charlotte and Wolf Leslau. Mount Vernon, N.Y.: Peter Pauper Press, 1963.

Twenty-five short and very short tales for young children.

African Folk Tales and Sculpture. Selected and edited by Paul Radin and Elinore Marvel. Sculpture selected by James Johnson Sweeney. New York: Pantheon Books, Billinger Series XXXII, 1952.

Kathleen Arnott. *African Myths and Legends*. New York: Henry Z. Walck, 1963.

Among other fine tales, a cumulative story of "Why the Bush Fly Calls at Dawn and Why Flies Buzz" (Eastern Nigeria) affords a good reading exercise.

Edna Mason Kaula. *African Village Folktales.* Cleveland: World Publishing, 1968.

Each story prefaced by brief description of people who live in territory. Many classic fables of interest to upper grades.

Harold Courlander and George Herzog. *The Cow-Tail Switch and Other West African Stories.* New York: Holt, Rinehart & Winston, 1947.

Tales of animals, kings, warriors, and hunters; of forests, the seacoasts, hills, and plains.

Harold Courlander and Wolf Leslau. *The Fire on the Mountain and Other Ethiopian Tales.* New York: Holt, Rinehart & Winston, 1950.

Symbolic tales of people and beasts mingling. Meaningful and amusing to older children.

Harold Courlander and A. K. Prempeh. *Hat-Shaking Dance and Other Tales from Ghana.* New York: Harcourt Brace Jovanovich, 1957.

Twenty-one short tales, thought provoking and full of humor.

Harold Courlander. *The King's Drum and Other African Stories.* New York: Harcourt Brace Jovanovich, 1962.

Tales from many different parts of Africa revealing many of the customs, moral values, and humor of African people.

Humphrey Harman. *Tales Told Near a Crocodile.* New York: Viking Press, 1967.

Stories of adventure and magic. Fine descriptive introduction of environs of Lake Victoria, the locale of stories. Wide interest range.

Virginia Hamilton. *Time-Ago Tales of Jahdu.* New York: Macmillan, 1969.

Geraldine Elliot. *Where the Leopard Passes.* Philadelphia: Dufour Editions, 1963.

Excellent collection of twelve tales appealing to all ages.

Adjai Robinson. *Singing Tales of Africa.* New York: Charles Scribner's Sons, 1974.

In his third book, Robinson retells tales that center around an African folksong with lyrics in the original language and in English translation. Stories about a giant, a wicked stepmother, and a mother-in-law make a novel addition to the usual cast of characters. Middle grades.

From Puerto Rico

Pura Belpré. *The Dance of the Animals.* New York: Warne, 1972.

Pura Belpré. *The Tiger and the Rabbit and Other Tales.* New York: Lippincott, 1965.

Ricardo E. Alegria. *The Three Wishes, A Collection of Puerto Rican Folktales.* New York: Harcourt Brace & World, 1969. In English; titles only in Spanish.

Reflecting a mingling of cultures—Indian, Spanish, and African—these twenty-three folk tales are set in a land of enchantment. Juan Bobo, simple John, outwits the clever; devils and witches lose to the virtuous; magic triumphs; and animals and humans seek adventures together. There are a number of cumulative stories but the style is generally fictional. Some stories for younger children; most of them for older.

From Mexico

Patricia L. Ross. *In Mexico They Say.* New York: Alfred A. Knopf, 1942.

Dan Storm. *Picture Tales from Mexico.* Philadelphia: J. P. Lippincott, 1941.

The tales in the two collections above bear a strong resemblance to African fables in depicting animals as principal characters and in

the use of familiar themes. Señor Coyote and Señor Burro, indigenous
to Mexico, appear as favorite characters in their local setting.

Camilla Campbell. *Star Mountain and Other Legends of Mexico.*
New York: McGraw-Hill, 1946, 1968.

A dozen or more poetic stories of nature and the supernatural
with historical facts and the true names of places and people inter-
woven with legend. Toltec Indians, Aztecs, and Mayas dominate the
stories. Good for fifth- and sixth-grade children.

From Creolean Islands

Harold Courlander. *The Piece of Fire and Other Haitian Tales.* New
York: Harcourt, Brace & World, 1969.

In twenty-six tales familiar themes are enacted by animals, men,
and gods featuring the humans, Uncle Bouki and Ti Malice.

From English-Speaking West Indies

Sir Philip Sherlock. *Anansi, the Spider Man.* New York: Thomas Y.
Crowell, 1954.

Sir Philip Sherlock. *The Iguana's Tale.* New York: Thomas Y. Crowell, 1969.

Sir Philip Sherlock. *West Indian Folktales.* New York: Henry Walck,
1966.

The Jamaican folk tales are typically African, adapted to the
local terrain. Anansi, the Spider (who can assume human form), tries
to outwit those who are stronger, sometimes succeeding and sometimes failing. Birds and animals of the West Indies take part in the
stories, most of which are based on the moral that fast, clever thinking is more effective than physical strength.

From the United States

Richard M. Dorson. *American Negro Folktales.* New York: Fawcett
Publications, 1967. Paperback.

A comprehensive collection of animal tales, Old Marster and John stories, supernatural tales, satirical anecdotes, and realistic reports of racial injustice. Bibliography and notes on recurrent themes of tales.

The Book of Negro Folklore. Edited by Langston Hughes and Arna Bontemps. New York: Dodd, Mead, 1958.

Some 200 pages of folk stories varying in degrees of sophistication furnish a wealth of material for a teacher's choice to read aloud. The wide range of subjects orients a white teacher to black folk customs and allows a black child to identify with the familiar ring of language and situation. As mentioned before, the Contents might well entice a child to try to discover something of interest in the body of the book.

Soulscript: Afro-American Poetry. Edited by June Jordan. Garden City, N.Y.: Zenith Books, 1970.

A collection of poems including some traditional favorites and others by young writers which upper-grade children will enjoy hearing read aloud and also enjoy discovering for themselves.

Tales and Stories for Black Folks. Edited by Toni Cade Bambara. Garden City, N.Y.: Zenith Books, 1971.

Original stories comprise the first part of this collection written on themes of living history that children can learn from their elders when they listen to tales told "in the kitchen." The second part, "Rapping about Story Forms," is introduced by an acute description of fables children can understand followed by rewrites of nursery tales in modern dress. Upper-grade boys and girls will especially enjoy the second part.

Harold Courlander. *Terrapin's Pot of Sense.* New York: Holt, Rinehart & Winston, 1957.

Thirty-one stories of animals and people gathered in rural areas from Negro narrators. Notes on the stories are particularly elucidating on subject of speech and also on the relation of these stories to folklore of other countries. For upper-grade children.

Children's Books

A Bibliography of Negro History and *Culture for Young Readers.* Edited by Miles M. Jackson, Jr. Pittsburgh: University of Pittsburgh Press, 1960, for Atlanta University.

Minnie W. Koblitz. *The Negro in Schoolroom Literature: Resource Materials for the Teacher of Kindergarten Through Sixth Grade.* New York: Center for Urban Education, 1966.

We Build Together: A Reader's Guide to Negro Life and Literature for Elementary and High School Use. Edited by Charlemae Rollins. Champaign, Ill.: National Council for Teachers of English, 1967.

Current catalogues from major publishing houses keep a teacher informed of new publications and visual aids. Many publishers have a department devoted to black and Latin-American resources. In addition, a number of minority-owned publishers specialize in these resources for the elementary school. Following is a partial listing:

Afro-American Publishing Company, Inc., 1727 South Indiana Avenue, Chicago, Ill. 60616

A publisher primarily of multi-media learning kits designed for classroom use or libraries, the company also offers historical posters, dramatized episodes of history on records or cassettes, filmstrips, transparencies, and other materials in a variety of kits.

Benefic Press, 10300 W. Roosevelt Road, Westchester, Ill. 60153

Publishes sets of three books for grades 2–4, 4–8, and 6–9 comprising a unified approach.

Buckingham Learning Corporation, 76 Madison Avenue, New York, N.Y. 10016

A publisher of multi-media learning materials in Afro-American history and social studies, the house also published *Dear Dr. King,* an anthology of children's writings on the murder of Martin Luther King.

Garrard Publishing Company, Champaign, Ill. 61820

> Offers high-interest books for grades 2–5 that include history, personalities; well illustrated.

Johnson Publishing Company, 1820 South Michigan Avenue, Chicago, Ill. 60616

> Publisher of *Ebony* and other black periodicals, the company offers several children titles and a series of reprints of black classics. One of its titles is Lerone Bennett, Jr.'s, *Before the Mayflower*, a history of American blacks.

New Dimensions Publishing Company, 151 West 25 Street, New York, N.Y. 10001

> Publishes five series of readers on subjects of especial interest to black and Latin-American children in the elementary grades. Two of the series are bilingual.

Children's Music Center, Inc., 5373 W. Pico Boulevard, Los Angeles, Calif. 90019

> A retail outlet for school musical equipment, they also have a catalogue of books and records for Spanish-speaking Americans graded from easy-reading picture books through those for twelve-year-olds. Many are bilingual.

APPENDIX II

Discography

A comprehensive Discography reflecting musical contributions of black Americans can be found in *Source Book of African and Afro-American Materials for Music Educators* by James A. Standifer and Barbara Reeder (Contemporary Music Project, 1972). Available from The Music Educators National Conference, 8150 Leesburg Pike, Suite 601, Vienna, Va. 22180.

Following is a list of a few recordings as examples for each category mentioned in this text. They are selected to be helpful in starting a small record library.

Afro-Rooted (with booklets)

Baba Olatunji. *Drums of Passion.* Columbia CS-8210.
Negro Folk Music of Africa and America. Folkways FE-4500.
Roots of Black Music in America. Folkways FA-2694.
Some correspondences between the muses of the slave area of West Africa and the Caribbean, compiled and edited by Samuel Charters.
Ray Van Steen. *Missa Luba.* Philips PCC-606.

Children's Albums (with booklets)

Negro Folk Music of Alabama. Folkways FC-4474.
Ring Games of Alabama. Folkways FC-7004.
Ella Jenkins. *Call-and-Response Rhythmic Group Singing.* Folkways FC-7308.
Calypso Songs for Children. Columbia CL-995.

Puerto Rican Dance Music
(plenas, bombas, controversias with others)

Paquito López Cruz y su Conjunto Típico. PLC-EF-901. Adrian Associates, Miami, Fla.
Ramito. A popular Puerto Rican singer who makes many records for Ansonia.
Songs, Dances of Puerto Rico. Recorded by Dr. William S. Marlens. Folkways FP-80/2.

Gospel Music

Best of Gospel, Vols. I–II. Columbia.
Golden Gems of Gospel, Vol. II. Peacock PLP-185 (ABC).

Blues

Anthology of Rhythm and Blues. Columbia CS-9802.
Roots of the Blues. Atlanta 1348.
Huddie Ledbetter: "Keep Your Hands Off Her." Verve FVS-9021.
Ray Charles: Genius Sings the Blues. Atlantic S-8052.
Bessie Smith, The World's Greatest Blues Singer. Columbia GP-33.

Soul

James Brown: The Popcorn. King S-1055.
Ray Charles: Man and His Soul. 2-ABC-S-590X.
Roberta Flack: Killing Me Softly. Atlantic SD-7271.
Aretha Franklin: Aretha's Gold. Atlantic S-8227.
Donny Hathaway: Extension of Man. Atco SD-7029.
Jackson Five: Greatest Hits. Motown S-741.
Sly and the Family Stone: Fresh. EPIC KE-32134.
Staple Singers: Be What You Are. Stax STS-3015.
The Temptations: An Anthology. Motown M-7823A.
Stevie Wonder: Talking Book. Motown.

Jazz

Art Blakey (drums). *African Beat.* Blue Note 4097.
Donald Byrd (trumpet). *Black Byrd.* Blue Note BN-LA047F.
Miles Davis (trumpet). *Bitches Brew ("Miles Runs the Voodoo Down").* Columbia GP-26.
Charles Mingus (bass). *Re-Evaluation: The Impulse Years.* Impulse AS-9234-2.
Sun Ra and His Solar Arkestra. *Heliocentric.* Worlds ESP-1014.

Partial list of outstanding black instrumentalists well represented on recordings:

Charlie Christian (guitar)
Ornette Coleman (alto sax)
John Coltrane (tenor saxophone)
"Slim" Gaillard (guitar)
John Birks "Dizzy" Gillespie (trumpet)
Billy Higgins (drums)
Milton "Bags" Jackson (vibraphone)
Thelonious Monk (piano)
Charlie "Bird" Parker (alto/tenor saxophone)
Max Roach (drums)

A few suggestions for outstanding Latin jazz instrumentalists:

Ray Barretto. *The Other Road.* Fania.
La Lupe and Tito Puente. *The King and I.* Tico-Roulette.
"Our Latin Thing." Fania.

Eddie Palmieri. Mango.
Willie Colon. Fania.
Mongo Santamaria. *Greatest Hits.* Fania 8373.

Concert Music

Afro-American Music Opportunities Association, Inc. (aaMoa)
is an organization dedicated to supporting black music and musicians
essentially in the areas of education, research, and performance. The
first of aaMoa's *Resource Papers* is a Discography of Concert Music
by Black Composers. It may be obtained by writing aaMoa Press,
Box 662, Minneapolis, Minn. 55440.

In cooperation with aaMoa, Columbia Records is issuing at
least twelve recordings featuring the works of twenty black composers. The first four recordings were released in March 1974; four
more will follow each year for the life of the series.

Black Composers

The Black Composer in America. Oakland Youth Orchestra, Robert
    Hughes, Conductor. Desto Records DC-7107.
Includes: *A Short Overture* by Ulysses Kay
    Passacaglia by George Walker
    Songs of Separation by William Grant Still
    Out in the Fields by William Dawsom
    A Quiet Movement by William Fisher
    Lullabye for a Jazz Baby by Arthur Cunningham
    Shapes for Orchestra by Stephen Chambers

Natalie Hinderas Plays Music by Black Composers. Desto Records
    DC-7102/3.
Includes: *In the Bottoms* by Nathaniel Dett
    Three Visions by William Grant Still
    Easter Monday Swagger: Scherzino by Thomas H. Kerr, Jr.
    Scuppernong by John W. Work
    Piano Sonata No. 1 by George Walker
    Engrams' by Arthur Cunningham
    Sound Gone by Stephen A. Chambers
    Evocation by Hale Smith
    Piano Piece for Piano and Electronic Sound by Olly Wilson

Selected Works by William Christopher Handy. Folkways FE-3540;
   Capitol SW-993.

Latin-American Music

Selected Compositions in Recordings of Basal Music Texts and in
   RCA Adventures in Music.
Ariel Ramirez. *Misa Criolla.* Philips PCC-619.

Electronic Music

George Balanchine. Electronics (Westminster). Includes "Music to
   the Ballet" and "Five Improvisations."
Sounds of New Music. Folkways.